Çatal Hüyük

NEW ASPECTS OF ANTIQUITY

Edited by Sir Mortimer Wheeler

Çatal Hüyük

A Neolithic Town in Anatolia

James Mellaart

15 Colour Plates
121 Monochrome Plates
56 line drawings

THAMES AND HUDSON

Contents

General Editor's Preface

THE PURSUIT OF KNOWLEDGE, like other human activities, is liable to proceed in phases, which may sometimes be described loosely and even cynically as fashions. Archaeology, the objective study of that human and therefore somewhat temperamental subject, Mankind, is not free from this foible. These 'fashions', however, are not merely a matter of whimsy; basically, they are often responses to advancing techniques and mark the intermittent and sometimes abruptly rising escalation of understanding. The present book, viewed in perspective, represents one of these upward steps.

Away back in the 1870's, Schliemann dramatically elevated the world remembered by Homer into a subject capable of material study. Troy, Mycenae, Agamemnon began to live not only in Homeric verse but in terms of battlements and burials which, in death and decay, gave a new life to epic tradition. This was the romantic era of archaeology. The detailed correctness of the new picture is not here in question; the broad likeness having been achieved, lesser men have filled in the hands and feet—it is their job. Later, Sir Arthur Evans in Crete began to paint in the prehistoric background of Homer and, with gradually advancing skill, depicted an imaginative dawn of Mediterranean and European civilization. The wider functions and capacities of archaeology were becoming plain for all to see.

But, unregarded by Evans, in the year (1900) in which the excavation of his Minoan Crete began, there died in Dorset a certain General Pitt Rivers who for twenty years, amidst the scrubby vestiges of prehistoric and peripheral Britain, had been quietly and industriously elaborating archaeological techniques. These, another twenty years after his death, were to begin the scientific revolution of his craft and were to lead, whether consciously or subconsciously, to the two decades of technical advance which marked the inter-war period. Between 1920 and 1940 there was a sudden blossoming of understanding. This included but was not confined to a new appreciation of 'stratification', a phenomenon already recognized a century earlier by geologists. It comprised also a general realization of the importance of environment in human progress; the recon-struction of the natural surroundings which, in great variety, had challenged Man and stimulated his advancement. The re-creation, for example, of vegetation and climate in various places and periods and on various soils was developed by the analysis of ancient deposits of pollen. Soil-maps and vegetation-maps began to give an enlarged meaning to human distributions, static or mobile.

And then, after the Second World War, there was another leap forward. New scientific aids of one kind and another came to the help of the archaeologist and threatened to turn archaeology itself into a science. At least they prepared, in anticipation, to turn the postulate of 'Two Cultures'—the sciences on the one hand as apart from the humanities on the other—into nonsense ten years before it was proclaimed at Cambridge in the Rede Lecture of 1959. Above all, in 1949 Libby's announcement of the radiocarbon (C-14) method of dating organic materials had given archaeology a powerful new scientific instrument for establishing a rough-and-ready chronology back to something like 50,000 years before the advent of writing, and so opened up a whole series of new horizons in the human achievement.

This ingenious by-product of nuclear research was promptly turned to good if sometimes unskilled use. It was now possible to interrelate cultures and civilizations intelligently with one another and with the present; ages unknown to history or to viable legend, and inadequately related by stratigraphy alone, took on a new mean-ing. Archaeology had indeed entered upon a fresh and revealing phase for which 'fashion' is a wholly inadequate term; to define it narrowly, the C-14 phase.

And the backward reach of the C-14 technique is happily sufficient to cover the most vital over-all period of human endeavour; that in which Man at last learned, in addition to gathering food, to produce it; thus almost indefinitely enlarging the potential size of the social unit and providing the essential basis of civilization, the ability to live in towns and cities.

In so far as the Eurasian zone is concerned, the focus of this greatest of all human achievements proclaims its own geographical terms. The wild prototypes of the principal Eurasian herd-animals (goats, sheep, cattle) and edible grasses (wheat, barley) occur or have occurred roughly between the Himalayas and the Mediterranean. Within that area, therefore, it may be supposed that the earlier attempts at domestication and cultivation took shape: always with the proviso that in other parts of the world—in the Western if not in the Eastern Hemisphere—equivalent advances may, at one time or another, have been independently achieved. And within that considerable Near Eastern and Middle Eastern region with which we are here concerned it is apparent that the earlier advances were liable to be located in the foothills; those, for example, of northern Iraq, Palestine, and southern Anatolia. This is altogether natural, since the circumscribed shelter of the semi-upland valley matched the size and capacity of the small societies which were still inevitably in the earlier stages of food-production. Only the confident development of food-producing techniques could be expected to result in a social expansion commensurate with the formidable problems presented by the great riverine plains.

And here Çatal Hüyük comes vividly into the picture. It lies upon an accessible and fertile landscape at a height of 3,000 feet above sea-level, and consists of two riverside mounds, the larger of which is 32 acres in extent. Thus by the seventh millennium, the age to which the earlier excavated strata are shown by C-14 evidence to belong, the settlement was of very substantial size, fully worthy of the urban designation which Mr Mellaart has given to it. As a fully-fledged town at that early date—three or four millennia before the famous cities of Mesopotamia—it is of more than professional interest. After its primary precursor, the eighth-millennium walled oasis-town of Jericho in Jordan, it occupies a sort of midway position in the emergence of Civilized Man. As such, it may fairly be regarded as something more than just another archaeological excavation; it represents an outstanding human accomplishment in the upward grade of social development, and may be expected therefore to be of general interest even to a modern age which may have lost something of the easy Victorian certainty of Progress.

The present moment is opportune for the publication of the results of the three seasons of excavation to which the site has been submitted. The first stage of the work may now be claimed to have ended, and some delay is inevitable before digging is continued. Meanwhile a reasonably complete presentation of the remarkable and sometimes bizarre results of the excavation to date is desirable in a form more congenial to the reader than the technical reports in *Anatolian Studies* can be expected to be. And there is ample material for this more general approach. Apart from the important contribution which Çatal Hüyük has made in the wider context of human studies, the idiosyncrasies of its inhabitants give it a personality of some special local and individual interest. The strange character of its closely packed buildings, into which in the absence of doorways the visitor presumably ascended or descended by ladder; the numerous shrines with their remarkable furnishings; and above all the curious and sometimes a trifle macabre artistry which doubtless reflects a religious thinking as involved and inscrutable as illiterate (if not literate) religions are bound to be—all these and other personalia combine to illustrate a community of an entertainingly esoteric kind. In one way and another Mr Mellaart's work is here offered as a notable contribution alike to the single-mindedness and the diversity of civilization in remote perspective.

MORTIMER WHEELER

Foreword and Acknowledgements

THE EXCAVATIONS conducted by the author at Çatal Hüyük from 1961 to 1963 with the generous support of a number of learned bodies in Britain, the Commonwealth and America have revealed a new and unexpected chapter in the history of Anatolia.

Çatal Hüyük has proved to be not only a major neolithic site, yielding rich evidence of a remarkably advanced civilization that flourished on the Anatolian Plateau in the seventh and early sixth millennium BC, but it was also the centre of art in a period that hitherto had been regarded as inartistic. Çatal Hüyük is remarkable for its wall-paintings and plaster reliefs, its sculpture in stone and clay as well as for its advanced technology in the crafts of weaving, woodwork, metallurgy and obsidian working. Its numerous sanctuaries testify to an advanced religion, complete with symbolism and mythology; its buildings to the birth of architecture and conscious planning; its economy to advanced practices in agriculture and stockbreeding, and its numerous imports to a flourishing trade in raw materials.

This book is an account of the first three seasons of work at this promising site and a summary of what has been learnt about it through the patient recording by a large team of archaeologists assisted by natural scientists.

The excavations were made possible through the generous support of the following institutions and benefactors:

The British Academy,
The University of London, Institute of Archaeology,
The University of Edinburgh,
The Royal Ontario Museum, Toronto, Canada,
The Australian Institute of Archaeology,

Christchurch University, New Zealand,

The British Institute of Archaeology at Ankara,

The Wenner-Gren Foundation for Anthropological Research, New York,

The Bollingen Foundation, New York,

The Ny Carlsberg Foundation, Copenhagen,

The late Francis Neilson, Esq.

W. J. Beasley, Esq.

The Earl of Crawford and Balcarres,

W. E. D. Allen, Esq.

and a number of anonymous donations.

Technical aid to the expedition was provided by the German Archaeological Institute, Istanbul; Shell, Ankara; BP (Aegean Ltd.) Istanbul; and the Conservation Department of the Institute of Archaeology, University of London.

The expedition has profited much from collaboration with natural scientists: Dr Hans Helbaek (National Museum, Copenhagen), palaeo-botanist; Dr Dexter Perkins, Jr, zoologist; Mlle Denise Ferembach (Institut de Paléontologie Humaine, Paris), physical anthropologist; Dr H. Burnham (Royal Ontario Museum), textile expert; Professor R. Pittioni and his team of metallurgists at Vienna; Mr H. Hodges (Institute of Archaeology, London), conservation and Professor A. Berkel (Forestry Dept, University of Istanbul) and E. Tellerup, Esq., (Copenhagen) for wood analysis. Other analyses have been carried out by Dr S. J. Rees-Jones of the Courtauld Institute, London (pigments); Dr G. F. Claringbull (Department of Minerology, British Museum, Natural History), Dr I. C. J. Galbraith (Department of Ornithology, British Museum, Natural History); the Rev. H. E. J. Biggs (Department of Malacology, British Museum, Natural History); the Radiocarbon Laboratories of the University of Pennsylvania (Dr E. K. Ralph), and the Centre National de Recherches Scientifiques at Gif-sur-Yvette, near Paris. Analyses of obsidian were made by Mr Colin Renfrew (Cambridge). The flint and obsidian industry was studied by Mr Perry Bialor and Mr Peder Mortensen.

During the excavations Mrs M. A. Mellaart and Mr Ian Todd were the photographers; Mr Peter Winchester, Mr N. Alcock and Miss P. Quinn the architect-surveyors; Miss Anne Louise Stockdale and Mrs Grace Huxtable the artists; and conservation was entrusted to Dr Hans Helbaek, Miss Fiona Greig, Mrs D. Biernoff and Miss Viola Pemberton-Piggott. During the summer and autumn of 1964 Mr H. Hodges, Miss M. White, Miss T. Martin, Miss P. Pratt and Miss V. Pemberton-Piggott worked on the conservation of wall-paintings from Çatal Hüyük in the Archaeological Museum, Ankara.

Archaeological field assistants at Çatal Hüyük included: Miss Diana Kirkbride (now Mrs Hans Helbaek), Mr Ian Todd, Mr D. Biernoff, Mr John Farrar, Mr Mark Davie, Miss Birsen Güloğlu, Mr Refik Duru and Mr J. Yakar. Mr Ali Riza Büyüklevent, Mr Behcet Erdal and Mr Hayrettin Solmaz acted as representatives of the Turkish Government.

It is a pleasant duty to express my gratitude to all these institutions, benefactors, scientists, scholars and assistants, who have thus contributed to the success of the Çatal Hüyük expedition and without whose support this book would not have been written.

We are not less indebted to the Turkish Department of Antiquities and Bay Rüstem Duyuran, then its Director and to Bay Mehmet Önder, the present Director, then Director of the Konya Museums; to Bay Rebii Karatekin, Vali of Konya and Bay Adnan Kızıldağlı, Kaymakam of Çumra and numerous other local Turkish authorities, for their help and assistance, hospitality and interest.

And finally, we thank our labour force, veterans of Beycesultan and Hacılar, or newcomers from Küçükköy, our foreman Veli Karaaslan and our *ustas* Rifat Çelimli, Mustafa Duman and Bekir Kalayci, for their skill, experience and devotion.

Preliminary reports on the Çatal Hüyük excavations have been published annually in *Anatolian Studies* (vols XII, 1962; XIII, 1963; XIV, 1964) as well as in the following journals: *Illustrated London News, New Scientist, Archaeology, Horizon, Scientific American, Science et Avenir,* and *Archaeologische Anzeiger.* An exhibition of copies of

Çatal Hüyük wall-paintings was held at the Institute of Archaeology at London; in the Jewish Museum, New York, and at the Royal Ontario Museum, and some of our finds have toured Western Europe with the exhibition of treasures from the Ankara Museum, where all our finds are kept.

Academic response to the Çatal Hüyük discoveries has been great and public lectures were given at Istanbul, Athens, Nicosia, Beirut, Amman, Jerusalem, Athens, Vienna, Berlin, Frankfurt, Marburg, Zürich, Geneva, Paris, Lyons, London, Oxford, Cambridge, Manchester, Leeds, Newcastle, Bristol, Edinburgh, St Andrews, Toronto, New York and Bryn Mawr. The need for a book on Çatal Hüyük is therefore fairly obvious.

I

Introduction

OUTSIDE THE RING of professional archaeology, Çatal Hüyük is still a name of little meaning. But the recent excavation of the site—still far from complete—has in fact given it an importance of an outstanding kind which it is the purpose of this book, during a pause in the field-operations, to indicate in a general way to a wider public. Already, after a mere three seasons' work (1961–63), the results may fairly be described as a spectacular addition to our knowledge of the earlier phrases of the human achievement in terms of urban settlement. For already Çatal Hüyük ranks, with Jericho in Jordan, as one of man's first known essays in the development of town-life. Before 6000 BC Çatal Hüyük was a town, or even a city, of a remarkable and developed kind.

The site lies 32 miles south-east of Konya in southern Turkey and will be described on a later page. Here, by way of introduction, something may be said of the general framework of terminology and technology which are assumed in the presentation of the results so far reached, together with a summary of some of these results in the Near Eastern context.

First, as to terminology. Traditionally the prehistory of mankind is divided into a number of periods, based on the typology of his tools and weapons in stone or metal: Palaeolithic, Mesolithic, Neolithic (Old, Middle and New Stone Age), followed by the Bronze and Iron Ages. This typology, devised in the nineteenth century for the prehistoric cultures of Europe, is now in many respects obsolete, but it is still in common use and has been adapted by Near Eastern scholars. However, as excavations have progressed and new evidence has become available, it has been found necessary to introduce more periods, such as Chalcolithic (a period in which the first metal tools and weapons came into use on a modest scale side by side with others in stone), and further subdivisions, such as a Protoneolithic, a Neolithic without pottery ('Pre-pottery' or, less committally, 'Aceramic') to distinguish these phases or cultures from others of a more developed Neolithic kind with pottery. Both the Chalcolithic and the Early Bronze Age have likewise been subdivided into subperiods, and with good reason.

Then as to the technology of dating. New methods of dating by means of the radioactive isotope of carbon (C-14) is rapidly providing a more nearly absolute chronological framework for prehistory all over the world, thus supplanting earlier schemes based largely upon guesswork.

A third factor of great importance is geography, for cultural development has been by no means the same all over the world, and regional differences can be extremely pronounced. Near Eastern archaeology during the last twenty years has disposed of the old cherished theories that all civilization developed in the Fertile Crescent, or, more simply, in Mesopotamia and Egypt. Botanists have shown that agriculture, the basis for the development of any civilization, did not start in the river valleys of the Euphrates, the Tigris or the Nile, but in the upland valleys, where the wild ancestors of the cultivated cereals had their natural habitat.

Subsequently to the Palaeolithic, two culture-provinces existed south of the Taurus Mountains, an eastern one in the Zagros Mountains and a western in Syria-Lebanon and Palestine. Anatolia has links with the western, not with the eastern group. This in turn suggests that there were a number of foci in the early development of civilization, and not a single one. Every year the study of the origins of civilization in the Near East becomes more complex and thus more human. Natural environment plays a decisive role in these early developments: people do not start sowing wheat in areas where this plant does not naturally grow, nor is metallurgy invented in areas devoid of ores. On the Anatolian plateau obsidian is abundant but flint is absent, so flint tools are rare: axes are made of greenstone in Anatolia, because this material is abundant, but in Syria and Palestine they are made of flint. To polish greenstone is fairly easy, but polishing flint is not; Anatolian axes are therefore always polished, Syro-Palestinian ones only on the cutting edge. Such differences in technique arise from the material and have nothing to do with date.

The mechanics of cultural diffusion are many and varied. There is a direct trade with one's neighbours, let us say across the rivers or the mountains, or that of the nomads whose recurrent and seasonal travel from one area to another makes them excellent culture transmitters. Another sort of diffusion comes when settlers move on to cultivate and colonize new territory, perhaps impelled by drought, floods, crop-disease, locusts or other pests, by soil-exhaustion, or population-increase. Whereas in the former instance time-lags are negligible, they may be pronounced in the latter. The spread of agriculture and stock-breeding from Anatolia to Europe is evidently a case of the latter form of culture-diffusion, marked by appreciable time-lags. A further form of diffusion leading to secondary Neolithic culture, in which colonizers with agriculture, etc., come into contact with, and transfer some features to, other people still in an earlier stage of development appears characteristic of Europe but is not yet attested in the Near East.

In Western Asia it would appear that there are at the moment at least three known centres where early civilizations developed in the postglacial period; the Zagros Mountain zone, Palestine and Jordan, and the South Anatolian Plateau. Of the preceding Upper Palaeolithic cultures much less is known in the Near East than in Europe, partly from inadequacy of exploration and partly perhaps because in this warmer zone open-air sites may have been more abundant than the occupation of caves and rock-shelters which help to guide the modern explorer. Not a single open-air site has been excavated, not a single Upper Palaeolithic statuette is known; wall-paintings have not yet been found, and engravings on rocks and pebbles or *art mobilier* are confined to one small area of the Near East, the region of Antalya on the south coast of Turkey. This is enough, however, to show that art both in its naturalistic and geometric form, existed during the Upper Palaeolithic in Anatolia in a region a few days' travelling from the Konya Plain in which the Çatal Hüyük civiliza-tion was to arise. The artistic production of the so-called 'Early

Natufian' culture of Palestine, immediately post-Palaeolithic, is well known and also points to Upper Palaeolithic traditions. Though less articulate the engraved pebbles and bone tools of the sites of Shanidar and Zawi Chemi, again of ninth millennium date, imply the same existence of such a tradition in the Zagros area. (Without detailed description or definition, these and other place-names may be sufficient to indicate the general shape and extent of the cultural problem in the light of present knowledge.)

In the tool-kit of the various Protoneolithic cultures (Natufian, Shanidar, Beldibi) there are numerous resemblances to the final Upper Palaeolithic cultures of the same regions (Kebaran, Zarzian and Belbaşi), but also enough differences to show that neither the Natufian, nor the Shanidar culture is descended from the Kebaran or the Zarzian. The Beldibi culture, however, looks like a development of its predecessor Belbaşi, and both are confined to the south coast of Turkey. If so, this is the only instance where a post-Palaeolithic culture can be derived from an Upper Palaeolithic one in the Near East.

However, archaeologists are agreed in regarding the Proto-neolithic and Neolithic populations of the Near East as descendants from earlier Upper Palaeolithic tribes of hunters who during the crucial Protoneolithic period (roughly the ninth and eighth millennia) invented and developed a new settled economy based on the domestication of plants and animals. Where and how this came about is still obscure but its importance for human development was such that the late Professor Childe named it the 'Neolithic Revolution'— a phrase which becomes less apt as our knowledge of the uneven and complex development of food-production (the process which Childe had principally in mind in coining the phrase) becomes a little more adequate.

Although the earliest domesticated plant-remains found do not yet much antedate 7000 BC (from the aceramic Neolithic at Hacılar, Beidha, Alikosh), the standard of domestication reached and the variety of crops grown presupposes a long prehistory of earlier agriculture which may well go back to the beginning of the Protoneolithic, *c.* 9000 BC.

Even if actual plant-remains have not yet been found, grinding-stones and mortars, sickles and storage-pits all suggest the beginnings of agriculture. Rock-shelters and the mouths of caves were still in use, but open settlements are known in the Natufian (Eynan, Jericho, Beidha) and in the roughly contemporary Karim Shahirian of the Zagros zone (Zawi Chemi-Shanidar, Karim Shahir, Ali Kosh). At Zawi Chemi domesticated sheep are attested around 8900 BC, which makes sheep the earliest domesticate. Hunting, of course, continued to provide the population with most of their meat. The purpose of animal-domestication was food-conservation and the production of milk and, in the case of goat and sheep, hair and wool. Fishing and fowling, the collection of roots and berries, mushrooms, snails, etc., evidently also added to the variety of foods available, and food was collected in baskets. Awls and needles of bone suggest skin-garments, and leather-working in general. Spindle-whorls do not yet occur.

The burials in Shanidar cave may belong to the Zawi Chemi settlement whereas intramural burial is well attested in the Natufian of Palestine. This difference in burial-habits between the two culture-areas south of the Taurus continues into the Neolithic: no burials were found at Karim Shahir or Jarmo, but at Jericho they are very numerous. In the Natufian of Eynan the use of red ochre with burials is widespread and there are numerous examples of frag-mentary or partial burials. Funeral gifts are common; necklaces and head-dresses of dentalium shells, or perforated gazelles' phalanges are characteristic of the Natufian. The Early Natufians belonged to an Eurafrican race (dolichocephalic) which may be related to the Upper Palaeolithic population of Europe and is widely distributed throughout the Near East.

Already in Early Natufian times a sanctuary was established near the great spring of Jericho. Somewhat later, still well before 8000 BC, people with a Natufian stone industry settled around the spring in flimsy structures and in time a small mound about four metres high arose as the nucleus of later Jericho. This period has been called 'Protoneolithic' and is still little known. Two important innovations may be noted in the stone industry: the first appearance of notched arrowheads, which indicates an early use of the bow, and the first import of obsidian, a black volcanic glass, used for the manufacture of tools and weapons. Recent analysis has established a Central Anatolian origin for this obsidian and we thus have evidence for trade with Anatolia perhaps as early as 8300 BC.

This small settlement grew rapidly in size and importance during the eighth millennium, the 'Pre-Pottery Neolithic A' period of Jericho. The houses were round, like those of Early Natufian Eynan but built of brick and domed, and soon the need was felt for fortifications. A huge stone tower with internal staircase, three superimposed city walls and a deep rock-cut ditch outside the wall introduce monumental architecture in the Near East. The stone industry, virtually unchanged from that of the preceding period and still microlithic is now accompanied by a fine bone industry. Pottery and stone vessels are unknown and containers must have been made of basketry, bast or skins. The obsidian trade with Anatolia continues. Burial habits betray Natufian origins, partial burials are common, groups of skulls occur, but the use of red ochre in burials, found elsewhere before and during this time, is not recorded. Anthropological research has established a new racial element, also dolichocephalic, but more gracile: the so-called Proto-Mediterranean, living side by side with the Eurafrican Natufians at Nahal Oren in Palestine in the final Natufian, contemporary with Jericho Pre-Pottery Neolithic A. Compared to the Early Natufian, these later phases appear to have been artistically uncreative. Towards the end of the eighth millennium Jericho was deserted and soon afterwards the site was taken over by a different cultural group, possibly the one against whom the massive fortifications of Jericho had been erected. A complete break in culture follows: the newcomers of this 'Pre-Pottery Neolithic B' period, which certainly covers the entire seventh millennium and may have lasted even longer, still knew no pottery, but made vessels of stone. Their houses were no longer round, but rectangular. Their bricks were different and larger, their plaster floors were covered with red ochre or haematite and polished. Circular mats covered some of the floors. A few buildings seem to have been shrines; clay figurines of 'Mother Goddess' type appear, but burial-customs differ little if at all from those of previous periods. A series of human skulls with features modelled in plaster and painted, and groups of human figures more or less naturalistically or schematically modelled but of almost natural size, belong to the later phases of the period and suggest cult-practices and revival of art. The stone-industry is a new one with fine arrowheads, tanged and often barbed, large sickle-blades, polished greenstone axes, but little obsidian. There is evidence for domestic goat, dog (?) and cat (?). At some stage of the period a wall of large boulders surrounded the settlement.

This culture is known throughout the Jordan valley and has links with the aceramic Neolithic of Ras Shamra in North Syria and Tell Ramad in South Syria, whence it may well have come. More remote parallels may be suggested with aceramic Hacılar (*c.* 7000 BC) in south-western Anatolia, where again we find rectangular buildings, red plaster floors and human skulls used in certain rites, but such features may have been widespread throughout these periods in the Near East.

The next development from aceramic to ceramic Neolithic is known south of the Taurus in its early phases only in Syria, at Ras Shamra and Tell Ramad, but has not yet been published in detail and its radiocarbon dating is not yet available. At Jericho there is a lacuna, probably of great length, and the evidence from other Palestinian sites is equally unsatisfactory.

At Ras Shamra on the North Syrian coast the aceramic period (V. 1) comes to an end *c.* 6436± 100 BC, and is followed (in V. 2) without any other appreciable changes in the culture by the introduction of a fine monochrome burnished ware, usually red and sometimes brown or black, apparently undecorated. With it are found a coarse burnished ware, rarely incised and a thick chalky white ware, crumbly and badly fired, which seems to imitate limestone bowls of the aceramic period. Another ware is coated with lime-plaster, perhaps a hangover from vessels in perishable materials, treated that way to make them impervious to heat. Both these latter wares soon disappear, but they are found at the beginning of the period at a number of Syrian sites, as well as at Byblos in the Lebanon. At Tell

Ramad in the south the sequence is similar, but a good number of burnished pots are heavily decorated like the Early Neolithic wares of Byblos which in my opinion may have been dated much too late.

What is particularly important is the fact that the fine monochrome wares of Ras Shamra, Amuq A, etc., clearly show their South Anatolian ancestry and appear in Syria at a date which is not far removed from the first appearance of this same ware on the Anatolian Plateau at Çatal Hüyük around 6500 BC. Other parallels may be established between Syria and Byblos and the South Anatolian Plateau in the obsidian and flint industry of this period and there is evidence for a lively trade in these materials at Çatal Hüyük.

This period of transition from aceramic to ceramic Neolithic, the half millennium between 6500 and 6000 BC in round terms, is essential to our understanding of cultural progress in the Near East, but it is still obscure in Syria, Palestine, Cyprus and Iraq, where the inadequately excavated and still unpublished small village-site of Jarmo, in the northern foothills of Iraq, appears to offer an eastern variant of this important transition.

The excavations at Çatal Hüyük throw abundant light on the civilization of a town of just this period in Anatolia and the great depth of the underlying deposits promises to yield evidence for the genesis of this remarkable civilization when excavations can be resumed. The wealth of material produced by Çatal Hüyük is unrivalled by any other Neolithic site. Moreover, not being a village but a town or city, its products have a definitely metropolitan air: Çatal Hüyük could afford luxuries such as obsidian mirrors, ceremonial daggers, and trinkets of metal beyond the reach of most of its known contemporaries. Copper and lead were smelted and worked into beads, tubes and possibly small tools, thus taking the beginnings of metallurgy back into the seventh millennium. Its stone industry in local obsidian and imported flint is the most elegant of the period; its wooden vessels are varied and sophisticated, its woollen textile industry fully developed. At Çatal Hüyük we can actually study the transition from an aceramic Neolithic with baskets and wooden vessels to a ceramic Neolithic with the first pottery. Abundant carbonized food-deposits establish the range of crops grown, collected or imported from the hills, the standard reached by agriculture *c.* 6000 BC, and the centre from which these crops reached Europe at the beginning of its Neolithic colonization. The animal-bones and the shrines show the importance of a new animal about to be domesticated: *Bos primigenius.*

As the dead were buried in the settlement, hundreds of Neolithic graves have been found, providing rich evidence for anthropological study. Funeral gifts, though not rich by later standards, are less sparing than among other contemporary cultures. Red-ochre burials are still found, and there is abundant evidence for secondary burial and excarnation (burial after exposure and the removal of flesh and sinews). Trade is well established and the main export was probably obsidian (and greenstone axes).

And last but certainly not least there is the evidence for Neolithic religion in the form of numerous shrines, artistically decorated with reliefs in plaster, either modelled on the walls or cut into the plaster when in position, or with wall-paintings in one or more colours, and covering a period securely fixed by numerous radiocarbon dates to the centuries between 6500 and 5700 BC. In the shrines were found cult-statues of male and female deities, carved in a variety of stones or modelled in clay and sometimes painted, predecessors of the series from Hacılar. Until the discovery of Çatal Hüyük there was virtually no evidence from the Near East wherewith to trace any possible connections between the naturalistic and geometric art of the Upper Palaeolithic of Europe and the first manifestation of art in the form of painted pottery and a few figurines of the Early Chalcolithic of the Near East, at least four or even five thousand years later. The current interpretation of Upper Palaeolithic art as an expression of hunting magic, a view borrowed from backward societies like Australian aborigines, etc., offered little hope of establishing any link with the later fertility-cults of the Near East which centre around the figure of a Great Goddess and her son, even if the presence of such a goddess in the Upper Palaeolithic could hardly be denied, which it is not.

The position has radically changed: Çatal Hüyük and Hacılar have established a link between these two great schools of art and a continuity in religion can be demonstrated from Çatal Hüyük to Hacılar and so on till the great 'Mother-Goddesses' of archaic and classical times, the shadowy figures known as Cybele, Artemis and Aphrodite.

At the other end of the scale much work remains to be done, but the archaeological, anthropological and artistic record of Çatal Hüyük is already strongly suggestive of an important heritage from the Upper Palaeolithic. A. Leroi-Gourhan's brilliant reassessment of Upper Palaeolithic religion (*Les religions de la préhistoire*, Paris, 1964) has cleared away many misunderstandings, and the resulting inter-pretation of Upper Palaeolithic art centred round the theme of complex and female symbolism (in the form of symbols and animals) shows strong similarities to the religious imagery of Çatal Hüyük; to such an extent indeed that ancestral Upper Palaeolithic influences may still be lingering at Çatal Hüyük, as they so obviously are in numerous cult-practices of which the red-ochre burials, red-stained floors, collections of stalactites, fossils, shells, are but a few examples.

The importance of the site of Çatal Hüyük, clearly stratified and easily datable as it is, for the study of art, archaeology, religion and technology of this vital period, contemporary with the generally miserable period of the Mesolithic in Europe, needs, I hope, no further emphasis.

Mersin

The ancient mound of Mersin, called Yümük tepe, lies on the east bank of the river Soğuk Su, some 2 miles west of the modern town. It was excavated by Professor John Garstang in the winter seasons of 1937–39, and 1946–47 (see J. Garstang, *Prehistoric Mersin*, Oxford, 1953).

The mound, an oval with a maximum length of 200 metres, covers 12 acres and rises to a height of 25 metres (over 80 feet) with approxi-mately thirty-three building-levels covering a range from the Early Neolithic, *c.* 6250 BC, to medieval Islamic. Whereas the later sequence, from the Early Bronze Age onwards, is rather incomplete and better attested at Tarsus, the reverse is the case for the early periods, the Neolithic and Chalcolithic, for which Mersin remains the Cilician type-site.

The first early site to be excavated in Anatolia, Mersin is important in that it offers the possibility of establishing links between the Neolithic and Chalcolithic of the Anatolian Plateau (Çatal Hüyük, Can Hasan) and that of North Syria (Ras Shamra, Byblos, etc.).

In the period with which this book is concerned, the Neolithic, Mersin was a fair-sized settlement, frequently rebuilt, producing pottery very like that of Çatal Hüyük, but often bearing impressed decoration. Its stone industry, in obsidian imported from the plateau, offers close parallels to that of Çatal Hüyük, but is more rustic in appearance. Local chert is also used. No substantial buildings were encountered in the trenches by which the Mersin Neolithic was investigated, and no traces of shrines or art were found.

Unless the limited excavations in the Neolithic levels offer a misleading picture, Mersin was a rather rustic village site with good craftsmanship in pottery and stonework but little or no sophistication. In this respect it greatly resembles the other Neolithic establishments in Syria, the Lebanon and Palestine, but clearly differentiates itself from the artistic people on the Anatolian Plateau.

Hacılar

A small Neolithic and Early Chalcolithic mound lies about one mile west of the village of Hacılar, 17 miles west of Burdur, on the Anatolian Plateau, roughly north of the Mediterranean port of Antalya. The site has a maximum diameter of about 150 metres and is 5 metres in height. Excavations were carried out there under the auspices of the British Institute of Archaeology at Ankara in the years 1957-60 by the author. The final publication has not yet appeared, but *Anatolian Studies*, VIII–XI (1958–61) contain the preliminary reports on the excavations.

The excavations revealed remains of three different periods: the aceramic Neolithic village, dating from *c.* 7000 BC; then after a long gap in occupation a Late Neolithic village (Hacılar IX–VI), dating from about 5750-5600 BC, followed without any break by Early

Chalcolithic occupation (Hacılar V–I), the main characteristic of which is a sophisticated painted pottery. The settlement came to an end about 5000 BC and the site was not reoccupied.

The main characteristics of these three periods are: rectangular mud-brick architecture with red-painted plaster floors, no pottery or figurines and virtually no finds (of small objects), except grain, for the aceramic Neolithic.

A highly sophisticated Late Neolithic settlement is Hacılar VI, with big houses, monochrome and some simple painted pottery, a fine series of statuettes in clay and stone vessels, bone objects, grain, etc. There is a rich Early Chalcolithic with monochrome and fine painted pottery, less naturalistic figurines, fewer objects but abundant food remains. Poor architectural vestiges mark Levels V–III, but there is a complete settlement in Level II and part of a great fortress in Level I. Considerable changes in painted pottery in Level I suggest newcomers with different techniques and traditions.

Links with Çatal Hüyük are particularly notable in the Late Neolithic pottery and clay statuettes, but diminish during the Early Chalcolithic.

II

The Site of Çatal Hüyük

ÇATAL HÜYÜK, one of the most ancient sites in Turkey, lies on the Anatolian plateau, nearly 3,000 feet above sea-level and 32 miles south-east of Konya. It is situated in the centre of fertile wheat lands, watered by the Çarsamba Çay which, emerging from the Lake of Beyşehir in the Taurus Mountains, flows into the Konya Plain near Çumra to lose itself in the salt steppe beyond Çatal Hüyük. The great double mound of Çatal Hüyük, which derives its name from a road-fork at its northern end, was built on an old branch of the river about a mile south of the village of Küçükköy, the headquarters of the expedition.

Fig. 1

Plate II

The vast plain of Konya is rich in ancient sites, but though a few were recorded by R. O. Arik between Konya and Çumra no systematic survey of the plain was made until 1951, when the author, as a scholar of the British Institute of Archaeology at Ankara, began his Anatolian survey with the Konya Plain. Although the mound of Çatal Hüyük was noted in the distance in 1952, dysentery and lack of transport prevented its more formal discovery till it was possible to complete the survey of the more distant parts of the Konya Plain.

On a cold November day in 1958, just before nightfall, the author, accompanied by Mr Alan Hall and Mr David French, reached the double mound of Çatal Hüyük. Much of the eastern (Neolithic) mound was covered by turf and ruin-weed (*peganum harmala*) but where the prevailing south-westerly winds had scoured its surface bare there were unmistakable traces of mud-brick buildings, burned red in a conflagration contrasting with patches of grey ash, broken bones, potsherds and obsidian tools and weapons. To our surprise these were found not only at the bottom of the mound, but they continued right up to the top, some 15 metres above the level of the plain.

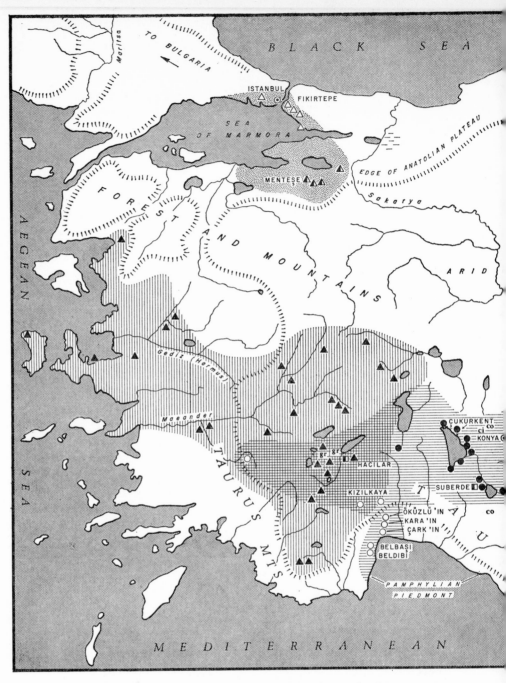

1 *Early Neolithic sites in southern Anatolia and North Syria and the sources of raw materials in the area*

The importance of our discovery was clear from the beginning, for both the pottery and the obsidian arrowheads found were strikingly like the neolithic material excavated years ago by Professor J. Garstang in the deepest levels of the site of Mersin, some 200 miles away on the southern Turkish (Cilician) coast. It should be remembered that in 1958 it was still widely believed that there had been no

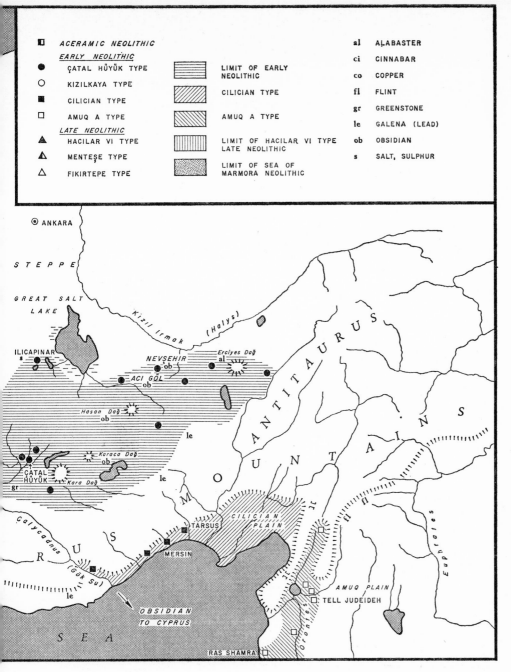

Neolithic habitation on the Anatolian Plateau. The mound at Çatal Hüyük provided eloquent proof to refute this theory, and what was particuarly encouraging was the huge size of the site (a third of a mile in length), the absence of thick layers of later occupation and the presence of a somewhat later mound on the other side of the river, which looked as if it would continue the sequence from

29

Neolithic to early Chalcolithic, just as at Mersin. Some of the painted pottery picked up there could indeed be linked to the latter site, but most of it was differently decorated.

Here then was a major site demanding excavation, but at the time of the discovery we were fully engaged by the excavations of Hacılar, a site near the lake of Burdur some 200 miles west of Çatal Hüyük. It was only in 1960 after a fourth season of excavations that virgin soil was reached over a large area at Hacılar and excavations ceased.

Excavations at Çatal Hüyük began in 1961 and were continued on a larger scale in 1962 and 1963, with ever-increasing success. In 1964, however, the excavation was interrupted and, instead, conservation-work was undertaken in the Ankara Museum by a team of specialists from the Institute of Archaeology of London University. The moment was opportune to evaluate the evidence and to summarize in this volume the result of three years' work at this site, and its bearing on the Neolithic development of Anatolia.

One of the main reasons for selecting Çatal Hüyük for excavation was that it seemed to fill the gap in occupation established at Hacılar between the desertion of the aceramic (non-pottery) village and the first arrival of the Late Neolithic people (*c.* 5750 BC) with a different and already fully developed culture. Earlier stages of the Neolithic, ancestral to those of Late Neolithic Hacılar, evidently existed and the site of Çatal Hüyük offered the best opportunity to explore such Early Neolithic cultures. Excavation at this site would also serve to fill the geographical gap between Hacılar and Mersin, and in view of the evident importance of the great alluvial plain of Konya Çatal Hüyük was expected to produce local peculiarities, different from the Neolithic of Mersin.

Plate 1

The main mound of Çatal Hüyük (the eastern one) forms an oval, measuring about 450 metres in length and 275 in width, thus covering about 32 acres. This makes it the largest Neolithic site hitherto known in the Near East. Its height is about 17·5 metres above the present level of the plain, and a small sounding has already established that occupation extends to a minimum of 4 metres below this point, without reaching virgin soil. The depth of Neolithic deposits at Çatal Hüyük (19 metres or more) is nearly twice that of Mersin

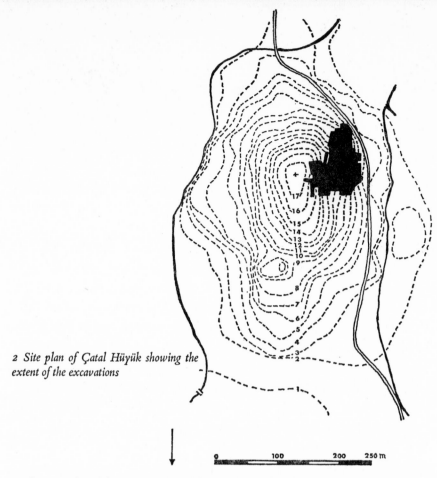

2 Site plan of Çatal Hüyük showing the extent of the excavations

0   100   200   250 m

and considerably more than that of Jericho (13·7 metres), and the reason for it lies in the fine preservation of a number of building-levels, where the walls of houses are preserved to a height of 2 metres or more.

Erosion has played its part in shaping the contours of the mound and it is clear that a considerable depth of deposit has been washed away by the rains and thunderstorms of the last seven thousand years. Of the topmost building-level (O) only some foundations remain; the floors have fallen a prey to the elements, and on the western slope the outermost rows of buildings show the same unmistakable signs of denudation.

The mound consists of a great central hump, steep on both long sides but fading gently towards the south, whereas at the northern end there is a secondary but lower hump. Along its eastern side lies a fairly broad 'skirt' of occupation now cut by the irrigation-channels which surround the mound; and from the occupation-debris

Fig. 2

31

Plate 2

Fig. 3

dug up from these canals it would appear that the 'skirt' dates from a fairly late phase of the Neolithic period, roughly corresponding to Levels IV–II on the top. Part of this low-lying area is covered by a modern cemetery, but the full extent of the site extends a little beyond the line of the irrigation-channels. On the western side, the foot of the mound nearest to the old river bed is under cultivation and a dust-track still in use prevents exploration down to the river-bed.

Excavations have been concentrated so far in an area of about an acre on the exposed western slope, where burnt buildings were visible even before the start of the excavation. Moreover, one would expect the earliest occupation of the site to have started nearest to the river. What sort of quarters and buildings lie on the other side of the mound or on the flat eastern 'skirt' we have not yet ascertained; but after three seasons of work it could appear from the gradual slope of the buildings towards the north and east that the original centre of the mound lies to the north-north east of the area in which we have been working. Although much has already been accomplished it is clear that this area alone cannot give us a complete picture of the structure of the mound as a whole.

No remains of buildings of a date later than the Neolithic have yet been encountered on the mound, but the upper levels of the site are badly infiltrated by brick-pits of the late Iron Age and the Hellenistic period. On top of the mound a pit of the latter date was found with bricks stacked for drying still *in situ*. Some of these shapeless pits are up to 4 metres in depth and cut straight through the underlying Neolithic houses and shrines. On the western slope, however, very few pits were found and the buildings are therefore better preserved.

It does appear from the area excavated that occupation gradually shrank in extent after building-level V, so that we were fortunate in obtaining steadily increasing ground-plans for the lower building-levels. It is possible that the occupation on the eastern 'skirts' dates from these later phases and corresponds to an eastward shift in the settlement, so that the total area of occupation in Levels V–I need not have been smaller than that of earlier levels.

1 The mounds of Çatal Hüyük seen from the north. Çatal Hüyük on the Anatolian plateau, 3,000 feet above sea level, lies 32 miles south-east of Konya. It is a double mound, the eastern neolithic one rising to a height of about 50 feet, covers 32 acres, whereas the western mound, its successor, is little smaller, but only 20 feet in height, and still unexcavated. Between the two mounds lies the old bed of the Çarsamba Çay, the source of the rich alluvial soils on which the neolithic people of Çatal Hüyük practised intensive agriculture. The now almost treeless plain was once covered with woods and parkland inhabited by Red Deer and wild cattle

2 Denuded mud-brick walls of building-level V on left and burnt and well-preserved rooms of building-level VI on right, on the west slope of the neolithic mound, looking south to the plain. The photograph shows the neat and regular layout of the rooms; one next to the other without

3 House VII.12 seen from the south-west corner. A classic example of the arrangement of platforms in a house with east-west axis with a single platform and bench against the north wall and further platforms against the west wall. The hearth is just visible to the right

streets or passages. See plan, *Figs. 7–9*. Hearths and ovens are easily recognized. When building remains are so denuded it is almost impossible to distinguish between houses and shrines having the same plans but different decoration

4 House A.III.10, the south-east corner with details of the oven in the south wall (bottom left) twice renewed, bonded brickwork and the diagonal mark of a wooden ladder set against the plaster of the wall. The position of the ladder, the oven and the hearth never changes in the buildings of Çatal Hüyük

5–7 Wall-painting, *above*, in red on white from house VI.B.65 the subject of which, though uncertain, may include the representation of ladders. *Below*, superimposed bread ovens of building-levels IV and V in a domestic courtyard, open to the sky. They are constructed of mud-bricks set on edge and their great size suggests a bakery rather than private domestic use. *Opposite, above*, hand and foot impressions in red paint on the east wall of house VI.A.63 near the porthole-like doorway leading to the kitchens. Such open doorways, never provided with doors, are found in most houses and one could only crawl through them into storerooms or other similar small rooms

8 Polychrome wall-painting from the north wall of shrine VI.B.1. This probably represents a mortuary structure, lightly built of bundles or reeds and matting, in which the dead were removed for the first stage in the neolithic burial rites, the process of excarnation, as is suggested by the human skulls and bones shown below

9 North wall of shrine VI.10, preserved up to roof-level, 11 feet above the floor of the building, the lower 2 feet are part of the original structure. Both floor levels show clearly in Plate 10. Note the characteristic overhang of the panels, the central post supported by a ram's head in plaster and the pillar of the bucranium on the platform's edge

10 North wall of shrine VII.10 below the decayed remains of its successor shrine VI.10 (*see* Plate 9), a characteristic example of continuity of cult at Çatal Hüyük. Less well-preserved is the central post and ram's head with a single horn and the plaster of the walls has been cut into animal shapes

11, 12 Examples of bulls at Çatal Hüyük. The fragmentary painting of a black bull, *above*, on the north wall of shrine IX.8 is seen through the doorway leading into the sanctuary from an antechamber. Only the legs and hoofs of a bull facing east (right) are preserved and to the left its hindquarters are partly obliterated by a cut-out figure of a feline head. The cut-out figure of a black bull, *below*, on the north wall of shrine VII.8, is two building-levels later, but in the same position as the figure above, and illustrates a further instance of continuity of cult. It is cut through nearly a hundred layers of white plaster but fortunately, not through the earlier wall paintings of the vultures (Plates 48, 49)

13, 14 *Above*, a baked clay model of a boar's head from a pit in Level VI. It is part of a figurine used in hunting rituals in which the animal was magically killed or disabled in effigy. The head should be compared to the cut-out in shrine VII.45 (*Fig. 27*). *Below*, the north wall of shrine VI.B.8 with a damaged figure of a huge cut-out bull in the same position as its predecessor in shrine VII.8, immediately below. There is evidence to show that this bull, more graceful than its predecessor, was alternately painted red and white and was less deeply incised. There were no wall-paintings below it and it lasted through both phases of Level VI

15, 16 The corner platform and the bench of shrine VI.61. This impressive building, evidently dedicated to the cult of the male god, symbolized in the form of a wild bull, bore no wall-paintings or reliefs. It was decorated with two huge bucrania set on the edge of the north-east corner platform, *above*, and with an even more impressive row of seven horn cores of *Bos primigenius* set in the bench at the southern end of the main platform, *below*. Six of these were at the same level and the seventh raised above it, like a serried row of stylized bulls' heads, one behind the other, in awesome splendour

17 Plaster relief of a stag from the north-east corner of shrine VII.10. Set in a shallow niche in the north wall, this relief was produced partly by modelling, partly in cut-out technique. Nearly three feet in height it shows a stag, perched on a rock turning its head backward, as if glancing at its pursuers, an attitude found also in the stag hunt in Plates 54, 55. and in the Late Neolithic theriomorphic vases of Hacılar VI. The left outline was produced by cutting away the plaster, the rest is modelled in low relief

18, 19 The Leopard Shrine (VI.B.44). The main panel on the west wall of this shrine was decorated with the bold relief of two painted leopards, the decoration of which had been repeated over and over again, so that finally there were nearly forty layers of painted plaster. One of the finest and best preserved is illustrated in a copy, *above*, and a detail of the right-hand leopard, *below*, shows the actual state of preservation. The burning of the two wooden posts between which the panel was set partly destroyed the animals and the hindquarters of the left-hand animal were carried away by **a** deep Hellenistic pit

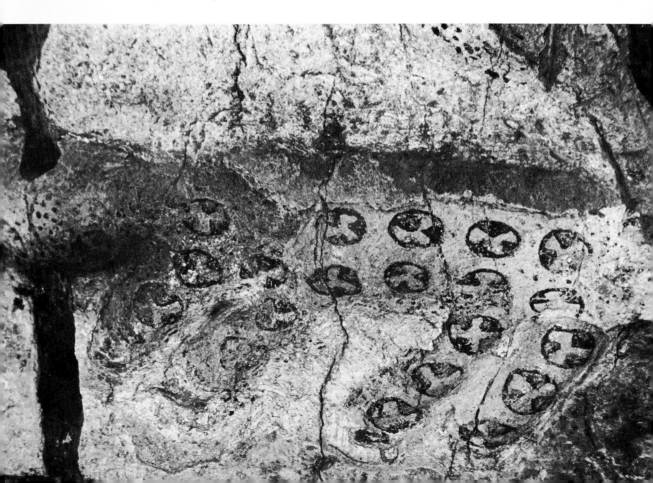

20, 21 The Leopard Shrine (VI.B.44). The entire relief, *above*, nearly six feet long was set above a red panel, flanked by painted posts. In its later phases, which may be assigned to Level VI.A, the painting became less naturalistic and the fine rosettes of the earlier phases were replaced by dots and dashes, executed in black (as before) but on a lemon yellow background, *below*. The eyes, mouth and the outline of the claws were still accentuated in red. As layer upon layer of plaster was added the animals gradually lost their crisp outline

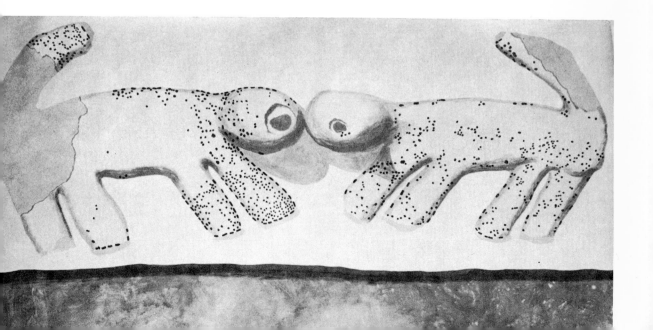

22–24 Bulls' heads in plaster, incorporating the horn cores of *Bos primigenius*, often of considerable size, are a feature of the west walls of many Çatal Hüyük shrines. Two bulls' heads of unequal size with red-painted ears and muzzles protrude from the right-hand body of the Twin Goddess in shrine VI.14, *above left*. Two others formed part of the decoration of the west wall of shrine VII.31, *above right*, the rest of which is lost. Earlier ones were provided with clay horns, *below*, and faced the relief of a goddess, with defaced head, in shrine VII.31

25, 26 Plaster reliefs of goddesses are frequent in the shrines of Çatal Hüyük VI and VII. Arms and legs are either outstretched, *above*, and Plate 24, or turned upwards and the latter indicates a position of childbirth, *below*. The lower part of a goddess figure from the north wall of shrine VII.45, *above*, resembles that of shrine VII.31 (Plate 24), but the figure on the west wall of shrine VI.8, *below*, is shown giving birth to a bull's head, placed below her legs (*cf. Fig. 23*). Goddesses giving birth are unpainted, the others are often 'dressed' in a bright colour

27, 28 Contrasting symbols of life and death are a constant feature of Çatal Hüyük. In the third phase of the decoration of the east wall of shrine VI.8, two rows of lower jaws of wild boar were stuck into the wall, to be covered in the next stage by womens' breasts modelled in clay. On the corresponding wall of the neighbouring shrine VI.10, *below*, a pair of woman's breasts each contained the head of a Griffon vulture (*Gyps fulvus*), the beak of which protruded from the open red-painted nipples. Beyond the post there was a horn in plaster, evidently a male symbol; and beyond the breasts a huge bull's head surmounted a red-painted niche

The Dating of Çatal Hüyük

Fig. 3

THE FIFTY-FOOT DEPOSIT of Neolithic remains at Çatal Hüyük, so far explored, has yielded the remains of twelve successive building-levels. These represent twelve different cities, not phases or repairs of single buildings. They have been numbered from the top (O–X) and there are two different building-levels in VI; VI A and VI B. It is possible that Level VII also consists of two levels, but this is not yet certain. Not all these were of the same duration and this is evident not only from the series of radiocarbon dates, but also from the state of the buildings themselves. Dwellings constructed of mud-brick are generally assumed to have short lives, but these vary from region to region and depend as much on the quality of the mud-brick and the solidity of construction, upkeep, etc., as on earthquakes, floods and the climatic conditions of the region.

At Çatal Hüyük each building had its own walls and was hemmed in by others, a method of construction which gave greater solidity to the buildings than they would have had if free-standing. Moreover, the inhabitants were careful to replaster their buildings continually, both inside and outside, a routine which materially contributes to the longer life of a mud-brick building by keeping out damp and rain, the main enemy of sun-dried brick. In the Konya Plain, the average annual rainfall is the lowest in Turkey, less than 16 inches (400 mm.), and most of the rain falls at two distinct periods, around May and November, in the latter half of the year often in the form of snow. Only the summer months are hot, dry and rainless, and to this day replastering is carried out after the rains of spring, to dry slowly during the summer. Weather-conditions allow for building and plastering but once during the year, and there is no reason to assume that conditions were essentially different during the Neolithic period.

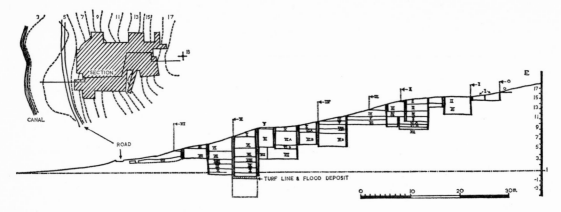

3 Plan and section of Çatal Hüyük showing the shifting pattern of occupation in the excavated area

At Çatal Hüyük in every room, both large and small, built-in furniture, walls, floors and ceiling, were coated with a fine tenacious white clay (*ak toprak*), found locally and still in use. The layers of plaster in each building can be counted and, though they are roughly consistent within each building-level, they vary considerably from level to level. This surely is an indication of the age of a building, the more so when one finds that those buildings that have been replastered most often (up to 100 plaster layers in Level VI B and up to 120 in Level VII) are in a poor state of preservation compared to those with thirty to sixty plaster layers which are well-preserved. In the former cases the buildings had become worn out; the plaster bulged, the walls were leaning at drunken angles, and they had become so dangerous for human habitation that they were condemned, pulled down and levelled. This was done by removing the flat roof and the beams on which it rested, by pulling out the wooden wall-posts which supported the main roof-beams, and by knocking down the upper parts of the walls until the room was filled with broken brick and plaster. In none of the buildings of the upper levels (VI A–I), where the wall-plaster is well preserved and relatively thin, is there evidence for deliberate demolition, but these levels had been destroyed by fire when the houses were still fit for habitation.

It appears then that with annual replastering the age of each house and building-level can be roughly counted and the maximum age to which a house was allowed to stand varied from a century to 120 years. Unforeseen circumstances usually shortened this excessive life-span, and on account of the frequent fires in the upper levels the rate of building increased considerably. Confirmation for the length of individual building-levels, as based on the annual rate of replastering, has come from radiocarbon dates. Counts of plaster layers then further help as a check on the accuracy of such C-14 dates and between the two systems a fairly reliable absolute dating can be established.

Çatal Hüyük and Hacılar are the only two sites in Anatolia which have been dated by a consistent series of radiocarbon dates, and the results shown on p. 52 are on the whole very satisfactory if one remembers that any of these dates may be a hundred years too early or too late; but a century is of little importance for the dating of cultures up to 9,000 years old. Most of the dates obtained come from charred timber (roof-beams or posts) in burnt buildings and thus date the cutting of the tree for the construction of the building in which it was found. Such dates give one the date of construction, whereas dates obtained from grain in burnt buildings give the date of the destruction, grain being never much more than a harvest old before it is consumed. Whereas grain cannot be kept for ever, timber (mainly oak and juniper at Çatal Hüyük) can and was re-used, and much of the wood from the unburnt Levels VII and VI B was evidently saved for re-use or for fuel. In this way it is possible to obtain dates which are far too early for the building-levels in which such old wood was found; *e.g.* in the case of the C-14 date for Level IV, 6329 BC±99, which may represent a post taken from a building in Level IX, or the 6200 BC±97 date which comes almost certainly from Level VII, although it was re-used in a building of Level VI B.

The radiocarbon dates from Levels IX and X, derived from the ashes of hearths, give only an approximate idea of the dates of those levels. Although the general sequence of radiocarbon dates is consistent, individual dates must be used with caution and they should not be dogmatically accepted if other evidence argues against their validity. Nevertheless, it remains our only method for dating

Chronological Table

HACILAR

	HACILAR		ÇATAL HÜYÜK		
c. 5000 BC	. . . .				
	I*d*				
	–I*c*				
c. 5250	I*a* *5247 ± 119*				
	II*b*				
c. 5435	II*a* *5434 ± 131*				
	III				
	IV				
c. 5500					
c. 5600	V				
	VI *5620 ± 79*				
	VII				
	VIII		O		
	IX *5614 ± 92*		I		
	→5706				
c. 5700		c. 5720			
		c. 5750	II *5797 ± 79*		
			III		
		c. 5790	*5807 ± 94*		
			IV *(6329 ± 99)*		
		c. 5830	. . . .		
			V *5920 ± 94*		
		c. 5880	. . . .		
			VI A *5781 ± 96*	destruction	
			5800 ± 93		
			5815 ± 92	beginning	
			5850 ± 94		
		c. 5950	VI B *5908 ± 93*		
			5986 ± 94	beginning	
		c. 6050/6070	VII *6200 ± 97* (?)		
		c. 6200	. . . .		
			VIII		
		c. 6280	. . . .		
			IX *6486 ± 102*		
		c. 6380?	. . . .		
			X *6385 ± 101*		
		c. 6500	. . . .		
			Pre-X floor levels (not yet dated)		

Radiocarbon dates in italic type.
→extreme tolerance.
All dates calculated with half-life of 5730.
Doubtful dates in brackets.

such early cultures and as the method gains in precision so will our dating gradually improve. The old method of guesswork-dating is no longer acceptable in scientific archaeology.

The fourteen radiocarbon dates then place Çatal Hüyük X–II between *c.* 6500 and 5700 BC in a space of eight hundred years and we may perhaps allow another century for Levels I and O. After 5600 BC the old mound of Çatal Hüyük was abandoned, for what reason is not known, and a new site was founded across the river, Çatal Hüyük West. This appears to have been occupied for at least another 700 years until it also was deserted without, however, any obvious signs of violence or deliberate destruction.

IV

The Architecture of Çatal Hüyük

Plate 2

IT HAS BEEN the purpose of the excavations to try to establish the lay-out of the architectural complex or complexes and so to obtain the maximum amount of information about the nature of this Neolithic city. Horizontal digging was therefore resorted to rather than vertical digging by means of trenches, which might give a stratigraphic sequence without much delay, but would tell us far too little about the nature of the buildings. Moreover, the presence of precious wall-paintings would not have allowed vertical excavation, and buildings had to be cleared laboriously one after the other. It is for this reason that virgin soil has not yet been reached anywhere on the site.

Although we have thus learnt much about the nature of the settlement and the ways in which these Neolithic builders planned their structures we have not yet succeeded in isolating a complete building-unit in the space of an acre, and these units appear to have been of considerable size. In building-levels VI A and VI B we have come nearest to this goal in locating courtyards and an outer wall round three sides of a vast block of buildings, but its eastern

Figs 8, 9

edge remains to be found. Of the later levels (V–II) we have found only the western edge and open space beyond, and of building-levels I and O little is still known, for their remains are either preserved only in limited areas (Level I) or are too badly preserved (Level O) to allow any statements to be made about the overall character of the buildings concerned.

In dealing with the architecture of Çatal Hüyük we are therefore obliged to concentrate on those building-levels (II–VII) which have

Figs 4–10

produced a coherent plan. The earlier levels, VIII–X, have only been tested in a few restricted soundings and they seem to follow the general pattern of building seen in Levels VII–VI.

Finally, the lower strata were reached at the end of the 1963 season in a test trench below the floor of a house of Level X which was only a metre wide and 3 metres long. Whereas this clearly shows that the occupation on the mound prior to Level X was at least 4 metres thick, the nature of the material was such as to suggest that we were dealing with at least ten successive plaster floors of courtyards at the western edge of the ancient mound and not with the remains of superimposed houses, unless these were of an altogether different nature.

All buildings at Çatal Hüyük were constructed of sun-dried rectangular mud-bricks, reeds and plaster. The bricks were formed in a wooden mould squared with an adze. Stone is not found in the alluvial plain in which the site was situated and for foundations up to six courses of mud-brick were used, well sunk below the level of the floor. The use of *pisé* or *tauf* was apparently unknown. Most of the brick was made with much straw, but in Level III sandy brick without any straw is also found and contrary to the well-known proverb it is of excellent quality. Most of the bricks are greenish in colour, but the sandy bricks are buff. A black mortar, rich in ash and broken bones (occupation-debris), was lavishly used, especially in the lower levels (VI) where the layer of mortar is often nearly as thick as the bricks (6 cms as against 8 cms). Bonding was practised.

Brick sizes varied and more than one size was in use in each level; the sizes are here tabulated:

Level II	Standard size:	65/67 × 37 × 8 cms
	Large size:	95 × 37 × 8 cms
Level III	42 × 25 × 8 cms	
	72 × 32 × 8 cms	
Level IV		
Level V	62 × 16 × 8–10 cms	
	92 × 16 × 10 cms	
Level VI A	Standard size:	32 × 16 × 8 cms
	Others:	32 × 22 × 9 cms
		38 × 12 × 8 cms

Level VI B Standard size: 32 × 16 × 8 cms
Others: 40+? × 24 × 10 cms
44–50 × 31 × 10 cms

The flat roofs were made of bundles of reeds with a thick mud cover on top and a mat below to prevent an incessant rain of bits of reeds falling on the floors. Two stout main beams and numerous small beams supported the heavy roofs. There is no direct evidence for the existence of a second storey of light materials or a partial second storey such as a verandah with columns, extending over part of the building, but some houses may have been provided with them. In any case some structure protected the light- and ventilation-shafts and the entrance-hole in the roof along the south wall. This may have taken the form of a hutch of wood provided with a wooden door, or it may have been a verandah or portico. That such protection was indeed provided is clear from the good preservation of the wall-plaster near the entrance-hole; this would not have been the case if the plaster had been exposed to the open sky.

Entry through the roof is one of the most characteristic features of all buildings at Çatal Hüyük; there was no other access to houses and shrines. But secondary rooms, used for storage, entry-passages or light-shafts, are entered from the main room through low open doorways, square, rectangular or oval in shape and up to 72 or 77 centimetres in height. None of these openings was provided with a door, and one could only move through them in a squatting or crawling position. Each house had a wooden ladder made of squared timber (10–12·5 cms thick), one side of which rested along the south wall, where it has left an easily recognizable diagonal mark in the plaster. This ladder led to a hole in the roof and through this same hole the smoke from hearth, oven and lamps, escaped. For this reason the kitchen end of the house, where hearth and oven are situated, is always placed along the south wall. To retain the maximum amount of heat, ovens (there may be more than one) are always set partly into the wall. They are oval in shape and vary in height, but all are provided with flat tops. Near the oven there is usually a deep but low recess in the south wall, which was evidently used for the storage of fuel (wood, brush or straw). The hearths are

Plate 7

Plate 4

Plate 4; *Fig. 11*

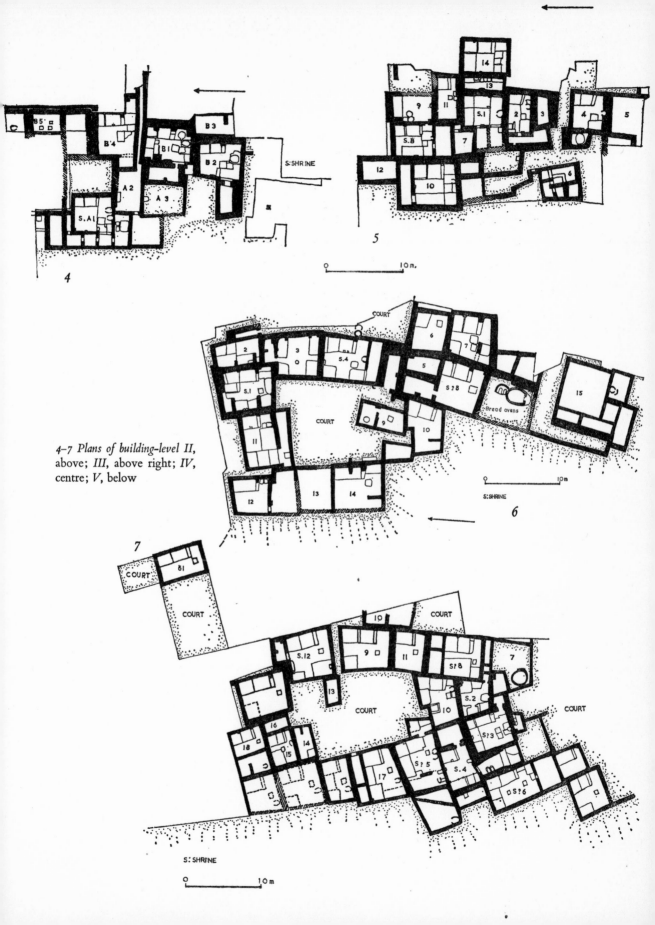

4–7 *Plans of building-level II,*
above; III, above right; IV,
centre; V, below

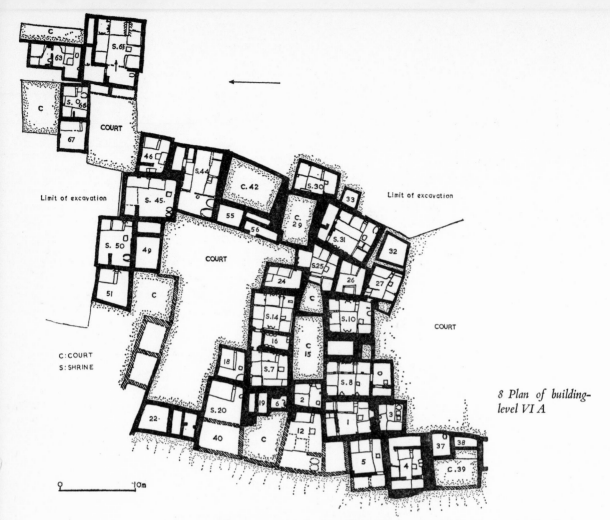

8 *Plan of building-level VI A*

rectangular or square in Levels I–VI B, round or square in the lower
levels, but they are always raised and provided with a curb to
prevent the spilling of ashes and glowing embers. It is unusual
to find more than one hearth in each room, and the kitchen part of
the house occupied one-third of the available space.

Raised platforms were arranged along the walls in the shape of an
L around the remaining square which was sunk and covered with a
mat. The usual arrangement of the platforms provides for a small
square platform in the north-east corner and a much larger platform
with a higher bench at the south end (nearest to the kitchen) situated
against the east wall. This was framed between two wooden posts
which were plastered and frequently painted red. One or more
subsidiary platforms are found against the north wall and still another
frequently occupies the south-west corner near the oven. This
arrangement is the normal one in buildings whose main axis is

Plate 3

Fig. 11

58

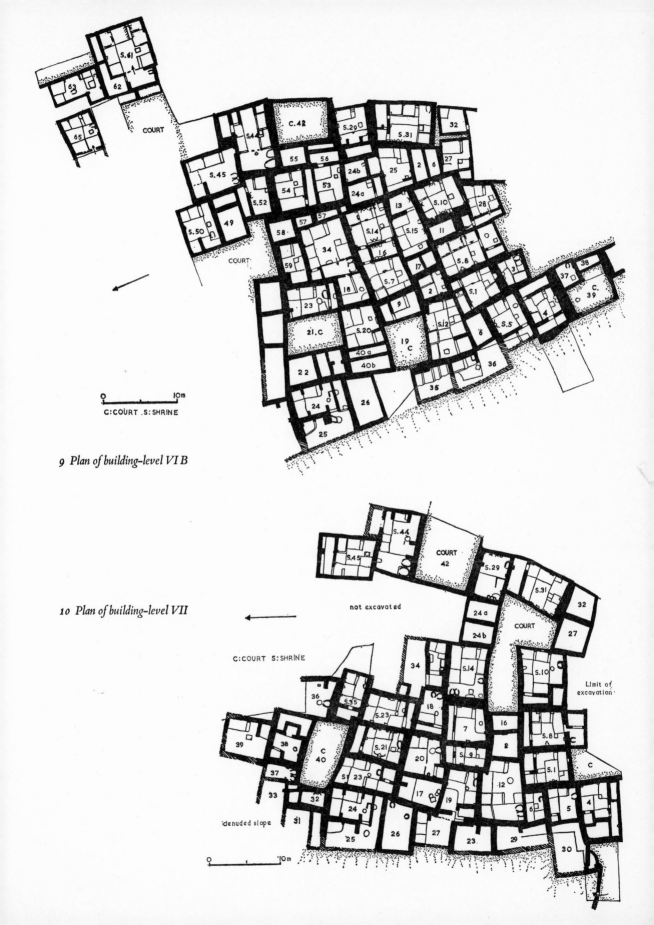

9 *Plan of building-level VI B*

10 *Plan of building-level VII*

S.61
63
62
65
COURT

C.42
S.29
S.4
S.31
32
55
56
24b
25
2
6
27
S.45
54
53
24a
S.52
13
S.10
28
S.50
49
57
57
58
S.14
S.15
11
34
16
59
17
S.8
3
38
37
S.7
18
2
S.1
C.
39
23
9
4
21.C
S.20
S.12
8
S.5
19 C
40 a
40b
36
22
35
24
26
25

0   10m
C:COURT .S:SHRINE

S.44
S.45
COURT 42
S.29
not excavated
24 a
COURT
32
24 b
27
C:COURT S:SHRINE
34
S.14
S.10
Limit of excavation
36
S.35
18
S.23
16
39
38
C 40
S.21
7
2
S.8 c
37
S.9
S.1
c
33
51 23
17
32
20
12
31
24
19
6
5
4
denuded slope
25
26
27
23
29
30

0   10m

oriented north to south, but in those buildings that have a west–east orientation the small platform is set against the north wall, though the larger platform and bench remain constantly set against the east wall.

These platforms, as carefully plastered as the rest of the house and frequently provided with rounded kerbs, are the prototypes of the Turkish sofa (and divan) and served for sitting, working and sleeping. They are often covered with reed or rush matting as a base for cushions, textiles and bedding. Below these platforms the dead lay buried, and from studying the burial customs it is possible to affirm that the small corner platform belonged to the male, the master, whereas the much larger and main platform belonged to the mistress of the house. The woman's bed never changed its place, nor did the arrangement of the kitchen, but the man's bed did. The sociological implications to be drawn from this are fairly obvious. Children were buried either with the women or under the remaining platforms, but they never accompany the master of the house.

From the bedding space provided by these platforms, which may vary from house to house and shrine to shrine, one can possibly make some calculations as to the size of a family. The main platform easily holds two adults, the corner ones a single adult or two small children. No single building provided sleeping space for more than eight people and in most cases the family was probably smaller. There is one house with but a single platform (A.III.13); there are several with two, but none have more than five.

The arrangement of sleeping platforms is not confined to houses but is also found in buildings which, on account of their interior decoration, served as sanctuaries or shrines. Here also the dead were buried beneath the platforms and hearths and ovens are found. However, for reasons to be explained later it seems unlikely that the shrines were continuously inhabited. What section of the population was entitled to live and be buried in the sanctuaries is of course unknown, but it would be reasonable to assume that it was the priestly class and their families.

It is evident from the wall-paintings in houses and shrines that there was a system of bringing light into the interior of these buildings

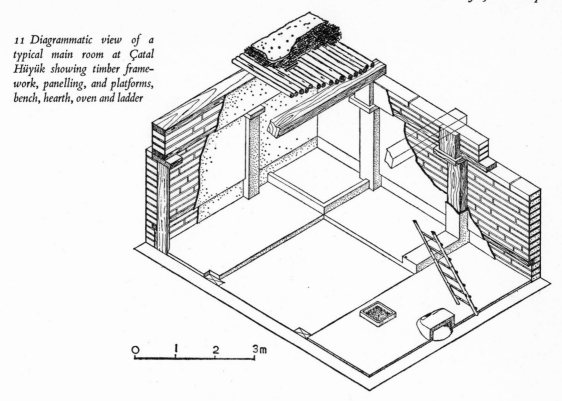

11 Diagrammatic view of a typical main room at Çatal Hüyük showing timber frame-work, panelling, and platforms, bench, hearth, oven and ladder

0   1   2   3m

other than that of a few stone lamps put in small niches in the wall. As the buildings rose up the slope of the mound in serried ranks, lighting would have been difficult but for the fact that each house had its own walls and its own roof level different from those of the surrounding buildings. By stepping the roofs light could be brought into the rooms through a series of small windows set high up in two of the four walls below the eaves (in the excavated area in the south and west wall, so that the light fell on the platforms along the east and north walls). It may be surmized that in buildings on the east side of the mound the windows were in the east and south wall and the position of the platforms was reversed. The position of the platforms is probably conditioned by the necessity of bringing light into the room and would differ according to the location of the building on the mound.

With the exception of occasional holes filled with sand or gravel set near the hearth, there are no arrangements for drainage in these

Fig. 12

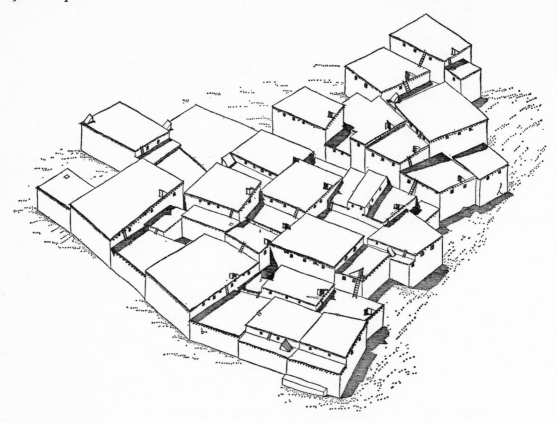

12 Schematic reconstruction of a section of Level VI with houses and shrines rising in terraces one above each other

buildings. For sanitation and rubbish disposal any open space, either courtyards or ruined buildings, were used and the thick ash deposits in these open spaces were efficient sterilizers. Houses and shrines were kept scrupulously clean; remains of meals such as broken bones are a rarity in any building.

Most houses have a storeroom and in some of these grain-bins of dried clay, about a metre high, were found in pairs or in rows. These were filled from the top and emptied through a small hole at the bottom (at floor level) so that the lowermost deposit of grain, most exposed to damp, was always used first. In other storerooms grain was stored in coiled baskets or in skins, but storage in pits lined with straw or matting, though common in later periods, appears to have been almost unknown. One is given the impression that each family baked its own bread, but in Levels IV and V huge bread-ovens with diameters of 1·5–1·8 metres and built of bricks set on edge were found in a courtyard which suggests a bakery.

Fig. 6

Other storerooms contained rows of clay boxes filled with knuckle-bones, stone tools, axes, polishing stones or sling ammunition, these latter particularly common in Levels II and III. Saddle querns and mortars are found in most houses and are often sunk into the ground, in contrast to the later practice at Hacılar where they are embedded in raised platforms to facilitate grinding.

A few houses have side by side with the usual oven another with a separate fire-chamber and a larger domed chamber than most ovens. These may have been simple pottery kilns. The domed chamber is always ruined which suggests that it was rebuilt for each firing and was completely closed during the firing process.

Survivals of Earlier Forms of Architecture

A further feature of the Çatal Hüyük buildings which is particularly interesting is the use of a timber frame in the mud-brick construction, which accounts for the characteristic panelling of the walls. In the earlier building-levels this timber frame is very pronounced (X–VI A) whereas in the later levels, though still present, it tends to become less conspicuous.

By pure chance the conflagration in which the settlement of Level VI A perished has led to the preservation of the entire north wall and the adjoining sections of both the west and the east wall of shrine E.VI.10, thus giving us the entire height of the building (3·3 metres interior measurement) and precious details about its constructions. The wooden framework was burnt out, but the baking of the brick walls has preserved its skeleton so that an accurate reconstruction can be made of the building.

Plate 9

Fig. 11

The most interesting feature of this construction is certainly the fact that the wooden framework could stand by itself, independent of the mud-brick walls. The brick filling (32 cms or just 1 foot thick) is awkward and of little strength and one can hardly escape the conclusion that the timber frame incorporates the main elements not of a brick, but of a wooden house, where the panels between the horizontal and vertical beams were filled with partitions of lathe-and-plaster or wooden planks. Peculiar to this wooden structure was a sort of corbelling, *i.e.* above each horizontal beam the walls are brought forward up to 23 cms, a feature that is not only decorative but originally devised to decrease the width of the room so that shorter timbers could be used for the roof-beams.

The origins of such wooden houses must be sought not in the almost treeless Konya Plain, but in the forest zone of the Taurus Mountains or their foothills on the edge of the plain. In the earliest levels of Çatal Hüyük it would appear that this type of wooden house was readapted to local conditions and thin mud-brick walls were substituted for the traditional lathe, plaster and wood panels within the timber frame. The result of this is that the weight of the over-hanging wall sections and the thick layers of plaster weakened the structure and when the wood rotted (as in Levels VII or VI B) or was destroyed by fire (as in Level VI A) the upper parts of the walls, left unsupported, toppled down without fail. The builders of Çatal Hüyük learnt their lessons, and from Level V onward they con-structed much thicker walls with larger bricks, greatly reduced the overhang and thus created structurally much sounder buildings. Gradually the emphasis on the timber framework was reduced and in Level II even the wooden posts were replaced by mud-brick pillars engaged against the wall. Thus internal buttresses were formed (the prototypes for the Early Chalcolithic ones of Hacılar and Can Hasan) and the framework retained only a decorative function.

The characteristic panelling of the walls at Çatal Hüyük is thus the result of the use of a timber frame, the elements of which are usually emphasized by the use of red paint. These panels in three super-imposed rows with the middle one at least twice as high as the two others, lend themselves admirably to interior decoration, such as reliefs or wall-paintings. In houses, as distinct from shrines, ornamen-tation was sparingly used and it was on the whole confined to the lowermost panel, varying in height from 60 to 80 cms above the main platform and the small platform in the north-east corner. The much larger middle panel is but rarely painted and the uppermost panels are never painted. Painted decoration in houses is found in several varieties; plain panels in various shades of red are by far the most common, geometric patterns, or hands or feet are much less frequent. More or less naturalistic subjects are mainly found in shrines, but there are some exceptions: birds decorated a central panel in house E.VI.B.44 and concentric circles and stars covered the same panel in E.VI.A.66. The well preserved buildings of the lower levels show that painting was widely practised and the comparative rarity of painting in the later levels is probably the result of the poor state of preservation rather than of a decline in this art.

Plates 5, 7

Another form of decoration, found both in shrines and in houses is the use of stylized bucrania which consist of a small pillar of brick in the upper part of which are incorporated the horn cores and the frontal of a wild bull (*Bos primigenius*), set on the edge of the main platform in a number of houses, to serve probably as a symbol of protection. In no single house was such a bucranium found intact and only the scars remain, but in sanctuaries the bucrania occur in multiples and they are frequently found more or less intact. It would appear that a single bucranium may be found in a house, whilst rows of bucranium are confined to shrines, where they may also be painted.

Plate 15

Evidence for still another sort of building comes from an intriguing wall-painting found on the north wall of a shrine in Level VI B (VI.B.1). The painting, about a metre long and 71 cms in height covered the lowermost panel and depicts a series of human skulls and bones below an architectural façade. A building with four gables separated by five pillars is represented in red and white paint on a buff surface, and the grisly remains of human bodies are obviously meant to be inside this building, which probably represents the charnel house where the dead were excarnated before burial in the settlement (see below, p. 204). The representation of the building is quite clear and it would seem to bear close relation to reed structures of the type still built in the marshy regions round the Lake of Eber (north-west of Konya); as also to the representations of reed huts in predynastic Egyptian art, and to the magnificent reed architecture

Plate 8

of the Marsh Arabs in southern Iraq. On the basis of these parallels our wall-painting would appear to represent a series of gabled rooms constructed of wood and matting with tall bundles of reeds forming the corner posts of these presumably rectangular structures. The binding of the reed columns is clearly indicated and so is the matting which forms the walls of the rooms. The flower-like crosses which crown the gables are probably stylized forms of the crossed bundles of reeds where they meet at the top, as in the Iraqi *mudhifs* and *sarifas*. The strange shapes which occupy the 'doorways' into the rooms may be interpreted as hangings and both the symbols on top of the tables (the quatrefoil) and the 'arm' on the hanging to the right may be intended to ward off evil. Both symbols we shall encounter on many other paintings.

If our interpretation of this interesting wall-painting is even approximately correct, we may assume that such charnel houses built of reeds were erected near the site of Çatal Hüyük for the first stage in the funerary ritual. But buildings of this nature suggest that other and simpler forms of building than those on the mound were still practised by the Neolithic people of Çatal Hüyük, if only in the service of the dead. As funerary practises tend to preserve archaic customs, we may well ask if buildings of this nature do not belong to earlier traditions than those we see on the mound of Çatal Hüyük, traditions which may well antedate the use of mud-brick houses which we now know did not start with Level X but were already used a millennium or so before. Monumental reed architecture of the type depicted in our wall-painting may have been characteristic of a period when mud-brick was still unknown and such buildings may have been commonplace at the beginning of the Protoneolithic period, *c.* 9000 BC, if they did not already exist in the Upper Palaeolithic.

Wooden houses and reed structures, vestigial remains of traditional architectural forms, have taken us back a long way into the still unexplored past of the Neolithic traditions of Çatal Hüyük. We must now return to our mound and see how these early builders planned their town.

V

The Town Plan

A MERE GLANCE at the plans of the various building-levels at Çatal Hüyük suffices to show that its builders were well aware of the necessity of planning an orderly settlement, far removed from the disorderly and random agglomeration of freestanding huts and hovels characteristic of the Protoneolithic period in Palestine, the only region where settlements of this period have been explored *in extenso*.

Orderliness and planning prevail everywhere; in the size of bricks, the standard plan of houses and shrines, the heights of panels, doorways, hearths and ovens and to a great extent in the size of rooms. Hand and foot seem to have been the standards of measurement with four hands (8 cms) to a foot (*c.* 32 cms); this is most clearly seen in the Level VI bricks which are one hand thick, two hands wide and four hands long ($8 \times 16 \times 32$ cms).

In the size of houses there are of course variations according to the family's need: they range from small ones with a floor space of 11·25 square metres to huge ones with areas of 48 square metres, but the most common size of houses and shrines varies from 25 to 27 square metres, *i.e.* rooms of about $6 \times 4 \cdot 5$ metres.

Houses are invariably of rectangular plan and the lines of the walls are as straight as the eye could make them. Storerooms and subsidiary chambers are arranged around the main rooms according to individual needs and their position is of little consequence. Most appear to have been lower in height than the main rooms.

Because of the habit of building one structure on top of the other, using the old walls as foundations a certain homogeneity of plan was created, but by subdividing rooms or joining others together, by using the site of one or more rooms for creating a courtyard or open space, the plans of individual building-levels vary considerably even if the general layout is to a great extent preserved. It will eventually be of great interest to trace the plans of the successive building-levels down to the original master-plan which the conservative builders of Çatal Hüyük continued to follow through numerous centuries.

The Neolithic builders were faced with a number of problems such as defence, communications between different quarters, terracing on top of an old mound, the arrangement of rectangular buildings to fit within the contours of an oval mound and the problems of providing enough light for the dense agglomeration of buildings, especially in the lower levels. This problem was solved by less congested planning which makes its appearance in Level VI A (compare the VI B and VI A plans) and continued in use until the end of the settlement. Access to these new courtyards was gained by narrow passages, open to the court, probably carrying a flight of wooden stairs that led to the roof. Wooden ladders facilitated access from roof to roof. The main use of the large courtyards appears to have been for the disposal of rubbish and for sanitation and they also provided more air, light and space. They were not used for keeping domestic animals in, nor for domestic tasks such as cooking or baking and no burials ever took place in the courtyards.

The need for defence may be the original reason for the peculiar way in which the people of Çatal Hüyük constructed dwellings without doorways, and with sole entry through the roof. Villages of this type are still found in central and eastern Anatolia, in the Caucasus and in the mountains of western Iran. Defence against potential enemies and against floods are the two main reasons for such a construction. A solid outer wall built of stone is the alternative, but stone was not available in the plain and floodwaters will eventually undermine any wall of mud-brick, however substantial. Moreover, the city of Çatal Hüyük was extensive and would need considerable man-power to man the entire circuit against enemy attack. Once the wall was breached an enemy would have been able to break into the city. The solution adopted at Çatal Hüyük was a different one: the planners did not build a solid wall, but surrounded the site with an unbroken row of houses and storerooms, accessible only from the roof. Even if an enemy succeeded in breaching the

Figs 8, 9

wall he found himself in a closed room from which the ladder had no doubt been removed with the defenders waiting for him on the roof. To take the settlement would involve close fighting from house to house in a maze of dwellings which would be enough to discourage the attacker. The efficacy of the defence system is obvious and, whatever discomfort it involved for the inhabitants of the city, there is no evidence for any sack or massacre during the 800 years of the existence of Çatal Hüyük, so far explored in the excavations. What any enemy might attempt to achieve was to set fire to the settlement, and so far no wells have been discovered, but it is also clear that the people of this city were sufficiently well equipped with slingshot, bow and arrow, lance and spear to keep any attacker well away from the foot of the walls. What caused the final abandonment of the settlement is still far from clear, but there is as yet no evidence for massacre and the new site across the river, where the inhabitants subsequently settled is nearly as large as the mound they had left.

The plan of Level VI B shows two terraces; an upper one with rooms in two rows (nos 47–32 and 52–27) and a lower terrace bordered by an outer range of rooms (nos 24–39) at the bottom of the mound. In this plan a great number of house-walls form a continuous line, evidently the result of planning blocks of houses and shrines as a single construction. Narrow rows of houses with an east-west axis alternate with broader rows with a north-south axis, but this principle has not been carried through to its logical end and pleasant irregularities break the monotony of row after row of dwellings and shrines. In Level VI A the complex of four shrines (nos 14 and 7, 10 and 8) is well balanced with courtyards in between and on either side, and a similar arrangement of shrines on either side of a courtyard is found on the upper terrace.

In Level VII rows of shrines alternate with rows of houses; in Level IV a system of courtyards is well developed and in Level III the main shrine is again flanked by long narrow rooms. Finally in Level II there are two clearly marked complexes, but these are only partly excavated. Between the two is a gate passage, which is better preserved in the previous building-level, III. The tower-like structure

Fig. 9

Fig. 8

Fig. 10
Fig. 6
Fig. 5
Fig. 4

north of the entrance passage was filled with great masses of burnt mud-brick which extended all over the surrounding area, suggesting that it may well have been a tower of greater height than the buildings around it. The original gate passage was narrowed by additional brick walls so that it was easy to block in case of an attack. The strange structure which lies immediately in front of it is not a house and marks a change in the original plan, being constructed at a somewhat later date. It obstructs direct entry into the settlement and may have served as a guard-house and the crooked passage which forms a cul de sac on the left while leading to a series of storerooms may have been devised to mislead intruders. The examples quoted show clearly that the builders of Çatal Hüyük did not construct at random but according to preconceived plans. So far no wells have been discovered.

Level	Total no. of rooms	Houses	Shrines	Proportion
II	5	4	1	4 houses to one shrine
III	9	7	2	3–4 houses to one shrine
IV	13	11	2	5–6 houses to one shrine
V	14	11?	3?	inconclusive
VIA	31	20	11	2–3 houses to each shrine
VIB	45	31	14	2 houses to each shrine
VII	31	20	11	2 houses to each shrine
VIII	4	2	2	Insufficient Evidence
IX	2	1	1	
X	2	1	1	

In the area excavated which covers about one acre—a mere thirtieth of the entire surface of the mound—a great number of houses and shrines with their storerooms have been found, but no workshops or public buildings. It must be assumed that these were located in a different part of the mound and the quarter on the west slope was evidently the residential, if not the priestly quarter of the city. One need hardly point out that Çatal Hüyük was not a village.

The proportion of houses and shrines in this quarter can be tabulated, as shown, but in this count the number of storerooms as distinct from dwellings is not included. From the table it might be concluded that there were more shrines in the lower building-levels, but two points should be borne in mind: (*a*) a much smaller area was excavated of the upper levels (V–II) and the shrines may have lain farther back in the unexcavated portion of the mound, and (*b*), in the badly denuded buildings of Levels IV and V the height of the preserved walls is often insufficient to detect such features as wall-paintings or plaster reliefs by which shrines are recognized.

I The twin-coned volcano of Hasan Dağ (3,253 metres or 10,672 feet) dominates the eastern end of the Konya plain and in clear weather is visible from Çatal Hüyük on the eastern horizon 84 miles away. Active until the second millennium BC it is probably this volcano whose eruption is recorded in a shrine of Çatal Hüyük VII, *c.* 6200 BC (Plates 59, 60). This view is taken from the north, along the Aksaray–Nevşehir road, with the Melendiz Dağlari, west of Niğde on the left. Hasan Dağ is one of the probable sources of the black obsidian used at Çatal Hüyük

II View of the plain of Konya from Çatal Hüyük, looking east towards the isolated mass of volcanic rock of Kara Dağ (2,271 metres or 7,451 feet) which divides the plain into two halves. Though not a volcano, Kara Dağ may have supplied Çatal Hüyük with the volcanic rocks used for querns and mortars, pounders and pestles, being only 22 miles away

III Shrine VI.14 seen from the east with storeroom (left) and shaft (right) entrances in west wall on either side of a monumental relief in plaster, a stylized double goddess with upturned legs of which the body on the right is giving birth to a large bull's head, surmounted by a smaller one. Arms and heads have fallen down in the destruction of the building, but one arm is shown on the floor (left). *Cf.* Plate 22, *Fig. 32.* Beyond the storeroom and shaft is shrine VI.A.7 (Plate V)

IV Shrine VI.B.8, showing the north wall with cut-out figure of a bull (top damaged by later building) and the east wall with small bulls' heads over the corner platform and rows of breasts, surmounted by scars of fallen bulls' heads above the main platform along the east wall. On the edges of the platforms are the scars of bull-pillars or bucrania. (*Cf.* Plate 14 and reconstructions, *Figs 41, 42*)

V East wall of shrine VI.A.7, showing beyond the projecting plastered edge of post the entrance to the shrine (in corner). In the centre of the picture is a red-painted niche and in the foreground the plaster head of a ram with the imprint of a red-stained hand, supported by a pillar of earth

VI Plaster relief of a pair of leopards from the north wall of shrine VI.A.44, partly destroyed by Hellenistic pits (left) or by animal burrows (centre). Placed above a red-painted panel, a couple of leopards is represented with the female on the left and the male on the right

VII Plaster relief of pregnant goddess from the east wall of shrine VII.23, richly painted in red, orange and black on a white ground. The head, hands and feet were deliberately demolished when the building was filled in, probably to rob the figure of its magic potency, a practise common at Çatal Hüyük. The goddess was richly dressed and the painting continues on the wall behind, as if she were holding an enveloping garment around her, the prototype of the later Near Eastern goddesses who show themselves to their worshippers

VIII Grooved and painted kilim pattern from the west wall of shrine VII.21. The grooves and the stitching along the top, imitating the sewn edge of the textile are in white, whereas the panels are alternately in black and red

I

II

III

IV

V

VI

VII

VIII

The Shrines and their Reliefs

THE NEOLITHIC CITY of Çatal Hüyük has yielded among many other splendours a unique sequence of sanctuaries and shrines, decorated with wall-paintings, reliefs in plaster, animal heads, stylized bucrania and containing cult statues, which give us a vivid picture of Neolithic man's concern with religion and beliefs. We have already seen Çatal Hüyük man as a builder, we shall now also recognize him as an artist of no mean stature, for the arts which he practised were manifold.

Out of 139 living rooms excavated at Çatal Hüyük II–X, not less than forty and probably more, appear to have served Neolithic religion. Such cult rooms or shrines are more elaborately decorated than houses and they are frequently, but not always, the largest buildings in the quarter. In plan and construction they are no different from ordinary dwellings and they include all the familiar built-in furniture, such as platforms, benches, hearths and ovens which we have already recognized as an integral part of the Çatal Hüyük building-tradition. Burials also are common in shrines, but there are some notable exceptions; none were found in the shrine of Level II or in the second shrine of Level III (A.III.8).

Although the decoration of the sanctuaries strongly suggests that these buildings were used for cult purposes, there is no provision for sacrifice. There are no altars and no tables for bleeding a sacrificed animal such as we find in the Early Bronze Age shrines of Beycesultan. Nor do we find pits for blood or caches of bones of sacrificed animals, and, with the peculiar construction of the Çatal Hüyük buildings, it would be impracticable to bring animals into the buildings for slaughter. If animal sacrifice was practised at all the slaughtering must have been done elsewhere and choice pieces brought down to be roasted on the hearth. Our only direct evidence for burnt offerings consists of small deposits of charred grain preserved between replasterings in red clay of a ceremonial hearth in the shrine of Level II. Offerings of other kinds which did not need burning are extremely common, and in all shrines small deposits of grain, tools, used and unused, pots and bone utensils, a few animal bones (perhaps meat offerings) bulls' horns, eggshells, gaming pieces, stamp-seals, in fact any acceptable gift, were found *in situ* as they had been deposited by the worshippers and preserved by the conflagrations in which many of these buildings had perished. The gifts varied from shrine to shrine: gifts of grain and legumes as well as stamp-seals were peculiar to the shrine in Level II; well over a hundred obsidian and flint weapons were found in shrine E.VI.A.14; piles of aurochs' skulls, horns and scapulae filled shrine E.VI.A.7; votive clay figures of animals and sometimes human beings were stuck into the walls of most of the Level VI A shrines in area E. Groups of figurines of animals: boar, leopard (?) stag, and cattle, used in a hunting ritual during which the animals were wounded or maimed in effigy, were found in pits near shrine E.VI.B.12 and E.IV.4. together with some intact weapons (lanceheads) and numerous clay balls (sling ammunition).

Such finds allow us to gain some insight into the many rites that must have been performed in these Neolithic shrines.

The main criteria for the recognition of shrines at Çatal Hüyük appear to be the following: the presence of wall-paintings of an elaborate nature that have obvious ritual or religious significance; plaster reliefs showing deities, animals or animal heads; horns of cattle set into benches; rows of bucrania and the presence of groups of cult statues found in the main room; ex-voto figures stuck into the walls; human skulls set up on platforms, etc. All these features do not occur in normal houses and the combination of several of them leaves one in little doubt that the building in which they are found was used as a cult room or shrine.

There are, however, a number of cases where the denuded remains make it extremely difficult to decide whether a building was a house or a shrine, and in most cases where there is doubt these are buildings which overlie an earlier shrine, and where a continuity of cult may be expected. That continuity of cult is a factor to be seriously considered is clear from a whole series of superimposed shrines often where there is no evidence left to regard a building as a shrine, the structure above it shows the unmistakable characteristics of being one, which strongly suggests that the sanctity of the place was remembered. There is some further evidence which may help to establish shrines; that of the eleven ochre burials found (Levels IX–III), six come from definite shrines, three more from buildings that have remains of reliefs and probably were shrines, and the two remaining from denuded buildings built over earlier shrines. It is therefore a possibility to be borne in mind that red-ochre burials only took place in sanctuaries. No single example has been recorded from a building that can definitely be described as a house.

Of the ten burials of women with obsidian mirrors (Levels VIB–IV) three come from shrines, two from possible shrines that also have ochre burials, two others from buildings situated above shrines, and three from buildings denuded to floor level. Although less definitive than the ochre burials of women, the burials with mirrors also show a connection with sanctuaries, and it is possible that both are associated with priestesses.

Belt-fasteners, made of polished bone, only accompany male burials in shrines and they probably served to fasten leopard skins, such as are shown in the wall-paintings. As it is unlikely that the entire population of Çatal Hüyük were so dressed, leopard skins probably denote a ceremonial garment of male priests as in dynastic Egypt. Carbonized remains of fur and skin, probably remains of leopard skins, have been found in a number of cases of male burials together with belt-hooks and eyes, but in others the material has not survived. Baked clay seals and metal are again far more common with burials in shrines than elsewhere but the evidence is not yet conclusive.

In a number of Level VI shrines the frontal bone and horn cores of wild bulls are set in a bench, but none are found in houses, unlike the stylized bucrania which are, on a few occasions, also found in ordinary dwellings. Likewise ram's heads frequently occur at the bottom of the post against the north wall, bull's heads are built into walls and a stag's head with actual antlers occurs once on the north wall of building E.VI.B.5, possibly another shrine.

Fig. 13

All these features as tabulated mark certain and possible shrines and it is therefore quite likely that our table of shrines and houses on p. 70 is in need of modification, as shown below;

Level	Definite shrines	Probable or possible shrines	Total of shrines	Houses
II	I	—	I	4
III	2	I	3	6
IV	2	3	5	8
V	3	4	7	7
VIA	11	2	13	18
VIB	14	2	16	39
VII	11	1	12	19
VIII	2	1	3	1
IX	1	1	2	—
X	1	—	1	1
	48	15	63	103

For those building-levels of which a sufficient number of buildings have been excavated (III–VII, excepting V) it would appear that for each two houses there was one shrine. In decoration as well as in size there are considerable differences between these shrines: some are obviously major ones and richly ornamented, and as major shrines I would regard VI:61, 44, 45, 31, 14, 7, 10, 8, 1; all of these have a north-south axis; whereas others have but a single wall-painting or animal head, and one cannot help wondering whether these lesser shrines were either subsidiary to the main ones, or the dwellings of a lesser order of cult personnel. Needless to say nothing is known about the Neolithic hierarchy, but the three groups of buildings in this quarter: greater shrines, lesser shrines and ordinary houses may all have been inhabited by various ranks in the Neolithic priesthood. It is not impossible that only the major shrines served the public cult, or were inhabited only periodically at the time of the great feasts, whereas the lesser shrines were the normal residence of the upper

Table of shrines and houses with their decoration and associated features (fig. 13)

Left table

Building-level	No. of House	Human figure	Bird	Hands	Kilim	Geometric patterns	Red panels	Bucrania	Red Ochre burials	Mirror
II	B II.1									
	B II.2									
	A II.5									
III	A III.2									
	A III.4									
	A III.9									
	A.III.10									
IV	E.IV.2									
	E.IV.11									
	E.IV.12									
	E IV.6									
	E IV.7									
V	E V.10									
	E V.17									
VI A	VI A.3									
	VI A.20									
	VI A.18									
	VI A.24									
	VI A.26									
	VI A.27									
	VI A.46									
	VI A.63									
VI B	VI B.65									
	VI B.54									
	VI B.53									
	VI B.59									
	VI B.34									
	VI B.28									
	VI B.25									
	VI B.18									
	VI B.9									
	VI B.24									
	VI B.36									
	VI B.4									
VII	VII.4									
	VII.5									
	VII.6									
	VII.12									
	VII.7									
	VII.19									
	VII.20									
	VII.18									
	VII.38									

Right table

Building-level	No. of Shrine	WALL PAINTINGS										PLASTER RELIEFS								BURIALS					
		Human figures	Bulls	Vultures	Stags	Goddess	Hands	Architecture	Symbols	Kilim/textile	Simple patterns	Goddess	Animals in sunk relief	Animals	Animal heads	Bucrania	Horns in bench	Fragmentary	Breasts	Red Ochre burials	Mirrors	Pits with clay figures	Cult statuettes	Metal	Position over earlier shrines
II	A II.1																								
III	A III.1																								
	A III.8																								
?	A III.13																								
IV	E IV.1																								
	E IV.4																								
?	E IV.8																								
?	E IV.10																								
?	A IV.1																								
V	E V.2																								
	E V.4																								
	E V.12																								
?	E V.5																								
?	E V.3																								
?	E V.6																								
?	E V.8																								
VI A	VI A.8																								
	VI A.10																								
	VI A.25																								
	VI A.50																								
	VI A.51																								
	VI A.66																								
	VI A.7									?															
	VI A.30									?															?
VI A & B	VI.31									?															
	VI.44																								
	VI.61																								?
	VI.14																								
	VI.45																								
VI B	VI B.8															?									
	VI B.10																								
	VI B.12																								
	VI B.7																								
	VI B.1															?									
	VI B.15									?															
	VI B.20																								
	VI B.5									?															
	VI B.23																								
?	VI B.29																								
?	VI B.52																								
VII	VII.8																								
	VII.9																								
	VII.10																								
	VII.14																								
	VII.21																								
	VII.23																								
	VII.35																								
	VII.29																								
	VII.31																								
	VII.45																								
	VII.1																								
?	VII.22																								
VIII	VIII.8																								
	VIII.1																								
	VIII.2																								
IX	IX.1																								
	IX.8																								
X	X.1																								

13 Table of shrines and houses with their decoration and associated features

14, 15 Reconstructions of the Second Vulture Shrine (VII.21) with human skulls as found.

priesthood, the houses those of the lower. All this is mere conjecture, but some such system would not be incompatible with the archaeological record. Only more extensive excavations can possibly shed light on the social structure of Neolithic Çatal Hüyük. In this connection it is worth noting that there is no relation between the size of a building or the abundance of its decoration and the poverty or richness of the burial gifts of the dead below its platforms. The only correlation that can be made is that burials in shrines are more richly equipped than burials in houses.

That wall-paintings and plaster reliefs of goddesses and animal heads had a ritual significance and were not purely decorative (or in the case of animal-heads substitutes for hunters' trophies) is shown very clearly by the fact that wall-paintings were covered by layers of whitewash after they had served their ritual function and that plaster-reliefs were made ritually harmless by the obliteration of the face, hands and feet when a shrine was abandoned. Many of the animal heads were similarly defaced or broken off and frequently only the outline survives or their original position is marked by a broad scar on the wall. Some of these heads were built into new walls, evidently to bring protection to the building. Only in shrines destroyed by a sudden fire have many plaster reliefs survived more or

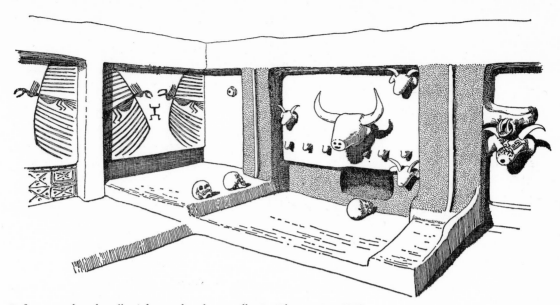

Left, *west and north walls*, right, *north and east walls. See Plates 30, 47, VIII*

less intact, but here the destruction has again obliterated the faces of the goddess reliefs. Thick layers of unburnt plaster cover the burnt hunting scene in shrine A.III.1 and the paintings of abandoned shrine A.III.8 were similarly treated. A further indication of the sacredness of the plaster reliefs is the small child's hand-imprint on the body of the goddess in shrine E.VII.23 and larger hands on the bull's and ram's heads in shrine E.VI.A.7. It seems that worshippers dipped a hand in red paint and left an imprint on the sacred image. The numerous panels with human hands in shrines (and sometimes houses) bear witness to similar practices on a large scale. Sometimes hands are found not on the bull's head, but around it (shrine E.VI.B.10.), and in one case there is an imprint of a child's foot (house.E.VI.63).

Plate V

Plate 7

If any further proof is needed of the sacred character of the Çatal Hüyük shrines, the unusual disposal of the body of a prematurely born child may here conveniently be mentioned. In shrine E.VI.A.14 was found a brick which broke and displayed the imprint of a bag. In it and carefully wrapped in very fine cloth were the ochre stained bones of a baby accompanied by two funeral gifts: a tiny bit of bright shell and a small chip of obsidian. This parcel evidently represents some hapless woman's offering to the Shrine of the Twin Goddess; more normal is the burial of a small child below the floor.

Even stranger is the collection of four skulls found on the floor of shrine E.VII.21. One of these lay in a basket below the bull's head on the west wall; a second lay below the bull's head in the centre of the east wall and two others were perched on the corner platform below the vulture painting. One gains the impression that these skulls were used in a funerary ritual, but as the graves in this shrine have not yet been excavated one cannot tell whether the skulls belonged to any of the burials in the shrine. In only one other building (E.V.6) was a single human skull found, in this case on the north-west platform. The presence of skulls in these buildings reminds one of the two skulls found propped up on stones on virgin soil in the aceramic village of Hacılar. Two others were found near hearths in later layers of the same village where no burials of the dead have been found. Some ancestor cult may perhaps have been practised at aceramic Hacılar, where it is considerably earlier than at Çatal Hüyük.

Religious Imagery

Shrines at Çatal Hüyük were decorated with wall-paintings or plaster reliefs, or both. Wall-painting was practised even before Level X, for a painted fragment of a doorway was found in debris on which a house of Level X was erected. Aceramic Hacılar also knew the art of painting floors and walls around 7000 BC. The custom remained in use at Çatal Hüyük at least as late as Level II, destroyed *c.* 5700 BC, but from this latest phase only the lower panels with plain red paint survive.

Plaster reliefs are just as ancient at the site and appear in the simple form of animal heads in a shrine of Level X, *c.* 6500 BC. Cut-out figures in sunk relief are first found in Level IX (in the form of heads) and entire animals cut out of the thick wall-plaster appear in Levels VII, VI B and VI A, sometimes combined with partial modelling of horns and eyes. Animals in low relief are found in Level VI B, breasts and horns from Level VII onwards and goddesses also make their first appearance in this level. Plaster reliefs were still in use in Level V, judging by a number of fragments *in situ* on the walls, but

29, 30 Among wall-paintings at Çatal Hüyük those imitating *kilims*, *i.e.* woven woollen rugs, are particularly common and are easily recognized by their intricate geometric ornament, their stitched borders and many colours. One of the most splendid examples, from the east wall of shrine VI.B.1, *above*, is painted in orange red, light buff, white, grey and black and contains numerous flower symbols. Another, *below*, in red and black from the north wall of shrine VII.21, combines painting with grooves and dots, left white, a style of decoration peculiar to Levels VII and VIII

31, 32 Of the two shrines of building-level III, one (A.III.8) is entirely decorated with patterns derived from kilims and textiles. A section of the latest kilim pattern in red, white and grey covering part of the north wall is shown in the copy, *above*, with fragments of earlier paintings showing underneath to the right. The continuation of this kilim pattern around the north-east corner of the shrine with only the triangles finished is shown in the original, *below*

33, 34 On the west wall of this same shrine (A.III.8) there were two main panels of decoration of which the northern formed the continuation of that shown in Plate 31. The southern, shown in the copy, *above*, and in the original, *below*, contained not less than four superimposed phases of painting: from top to bottom; the unfinished kilim pattern with triangles; the bold rows of quatrefoils; the finer quartrefoils and the step patterns. Each was separated from the other by a layer of white plaster

35, 36 Besides patterns that are obviously borrowed from textiles there are others, *above*, that appear to derive from leopard skins with the familiar spots (*cf.* Plate 18). Such paintings were only found on the south wall of shrine VI.B.1. A different pattern, *below*, from the edge of the doorway in the north wall of shrine VII.8 (see Plate 48) has a row of orange flowers and a mauve pattern reminiscent of fine basketry or matting

37, 38 Shrine VI.A.50 was decorated with another very fine kilim pattern, delicately executed in red, black and white on buff. Even its border is preserved. It shows close resemblances to the kilim pattern of Plate 29, which is a little earlier in date. Symbols include horns, flowers and even a small hand. *Above* is a detail of the burnt painting, with a copy, *below*

39, 40 The east wall of shrine VI.A.66, the smallest found, had a large bull's head with red mouth, ears and hair, but no actual horns, set above the bench. North of it was a panel of painting with elaborate symbols, painted in orange, white and mauve and a group of small red figures, including a woman, an archer and several goddesses in the posture of childbirth with raised arms and legs. A detail of the upper right portion of this panel in its original state is shown *above*, and a copy of the entire panel *below*

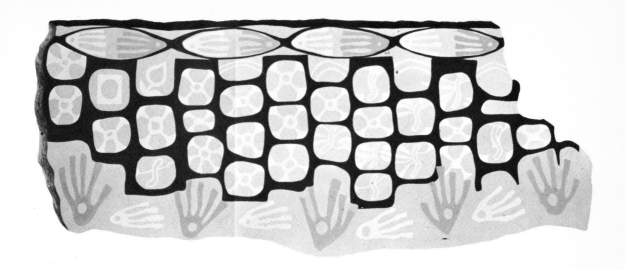

41, 42 Two superimposed paintings, of which the later, *above*, is only partly preserved, but the lower, *below*, more or less complete, rose above a lower panel with white hands left in reserve on a red ground above the central platform of shrine VI.B.8. Two rows of four-fingered black and red, grey and pink hands, the upper row encased in ovals, the lower alternately vertical or horizontal, frame a red honeycomb pattern. On this pattern is depicted, in both paintings, insects and grubs on a field of stylized flowers, *above*. In the lower painting the cells are closed on the left and open up in the centre; the painting might depict the life cycle of the bee

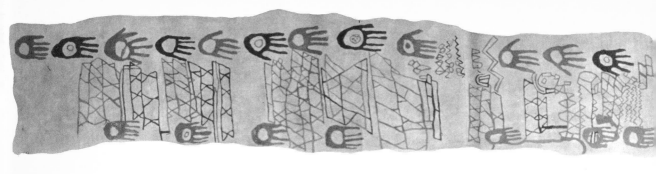

43-45 Around the north-west corner of shrine VII.8 there is an earlier panel of red and black hands above, (a copy *above*), and red hands below, (original *below*), framing a set of patterns that probably represent nets painted in red. *Opposite* is a gruesome scene of an enormous vulture attacking two small headless human figures, one of which is outstretched, the other crouched, like the dead, on its left side. This scene, from the central panel of the east wall, is part of a vast painting that formed the principle decoration of the earliest phase of shrine VII.8. Other scenes are shown in Plates 48, 49

46, 47 Shrine VIII.8, the predecessor of the Vulture Shrine, VII.8, similarly contained a painting of black vultures, unfortunately badly damaged, *above*. Here the scene is different for though a headless body lies between the two birds of prey, a man armed with a sling is actually warding off their attacks. Yet a third building, the Second Vulture Shrine, VII.21, contained scenes of this sort on its north wall. Between two of these creatures, provided with human legs, and perhaps priestesses or priests in disguise, lies another headless corpse, *below*, but in a position different from the others

48, 49 Although somewhat smaller in size, not less than five vultures pecking at headless corpses graced the north wall of shrine VII.8, where they were later covered by the cut-out figure of the black bull (Plate 12). These scenes probably indicate that the people of Çatal Hüyük exposed their dead to the vultures for the purpose of excarnation. A detail is shown *above* and a copy of the whole scene *below*

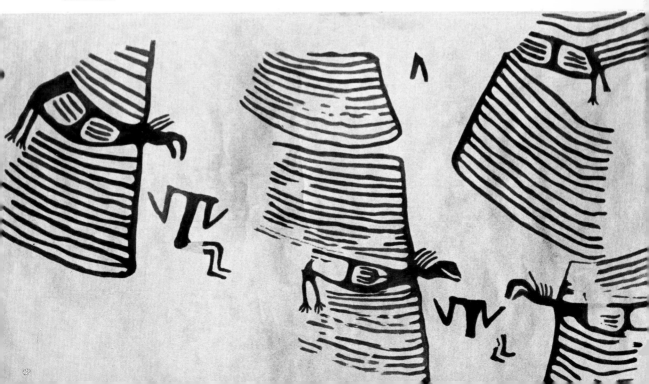

50, 51 Detail of a dead man's head, *above*, from the painting of funeral rite (?) *below*, on the south end of the east wall of shrine E.IV.1., the worst preserved of all shrines. The black-haired and bearded head with closed eyes, red smeared brow and gaping mouth may have been carried by a figure of which only the torso is preserved

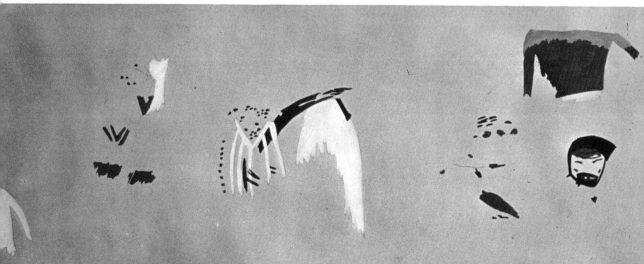

52, 53 Detail of a small white 'Goddess', *below*, from the continuation of the wall-painting (Plate 51) on the east wall of shrine E.IV.1. *Above*, a fragmentary painting with long-headed, running figures and a bull (?) partly obscured by remains of overpainting from the central post on the north wall of building A.IV.1

54, 55 Monochrome red painting of a deer hunt, *above*, from the truncated south wall of the ante-chamber to shrine A.III.1. Six male figures pursue a herd of Red Deer (*Cervus elaphus*), one of which has been brought to its knees by two men, *below*, and turns its head towards its attackers, while the others attempt to escape

56, 57 Monochrome red painting of a deer hunt from the north wall of room A.III.13. A stag and its young are pursued by an archer accompanied by his dog, one of the earliest representations of this domestic animal. The archer has just released his arrow

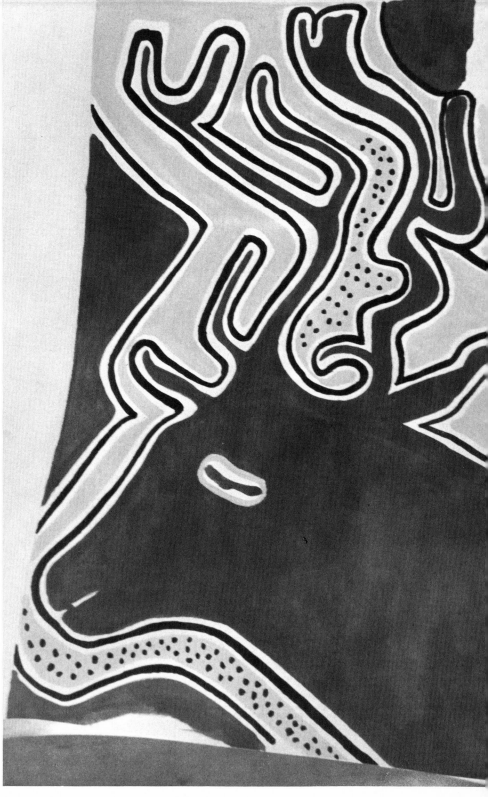

58 Tentative reconstruction of a stag's head, painted in red, black and white on the north side of the niche in the east wall of shrine A.III.1

none have been found in Levels IV–I and it may be assumed that this method of decoration had gone out of use.

Benches decorated with horns, which may be interpreted as a stylized form of a row of bulls' heads placed one behind the other are confined to Levels VI B and VI A, but the simpler form, the bucranium, first found in Level VII, continued in use till the end of Level II.

In plaster reliefs goddesses appear solely in anthropomorphic form and the place of the male is taken by bulls and rams, a more impressive exponent of male fertility. Only the bull, the stag and the leopard occur in full outline as well as in the form of heads, whereas the ram is never fully shown, and is simply represented by ram's heads. Stags, boar and leopards are rare and may be regarded as attributes of the deities, rather than as symbols of the god and goddess themselves. In the earlier animal heads the horns are usually modelled in clay and plaster, but from Level VII onwards the use of the actual horn cores and frontal bones of dead animals is found on a great scale in Levels VI B and VI A. So far other animals, such as vultures, other birds or dogs are only found in the wall-paintings or carved in stone. Snake and goat are conspicuous by their absence.

Plaster reliefs are frequently painted and the two techniques are evidently complementary. Whereas the animal heads are solid and moulded in clay covered with plaster, the large figures of goddesses were made of plaster moulded on bundles of reeds, the imprint of which is frequently preserved, or on wooden posts, preserved by carbonization. Many animal-heads were likewise set in superimposed rows on posts (especially in Level VII) or they were fixed on to the lower end of a post. In other cases single horns were used to attach the animal head to the wall. Whereas animal bones, horns, etc., were used for attachment and horn cores were used to enhance a naturalistic representation of the animal, the lower jaws of gigantic wild boar were stuck in rows into the walls of certain shrines, and these as well as the skulls of vultures, foxes and weasels, found in the representations of breasts, evidently have a ritual and symbolic meaning of their own. They serve no technical function.

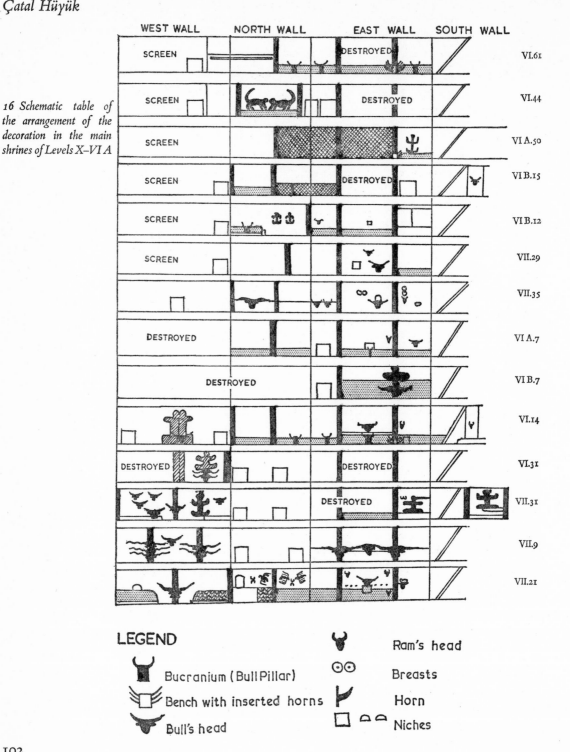

16 *Schematic table of the arrangement of the decoration in the main shrines of Levels X–VI A*

LEGEND

Bucranium (Bull Pillar)

Bench with inserted horns

Bull's head

Ram's head

Breasts

Horn

Niches

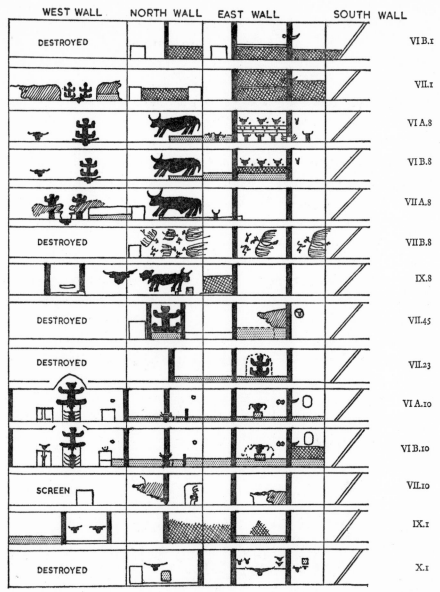

WEST WALL	NORTH WALL	EAST WALL	SOUTH WALL	
DESTROYED				VI B.1
				VII.1
				VI A.8
				VI B.8
				VII A.8
DESTROYED				VII B.8
				IX.8
DESTROYED				VII.45
DESTROYED				VII.23
				VI A.10
				VI B.10
SCREEN				VII.10
				IX.1
DESTROYED				X.1

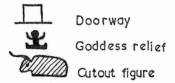

Doorway

Goddess relief

Cutout figure

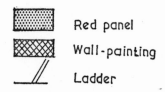

Red panel

Wall-painting

Ladder

Fig. 16

The diagrammatic table on pages 102–3 shows the arrangement of the decoration in the best preserved twenty-eight shrines of Levels X–VIA. It appears that the decoration of shrines followed certain rules; scenes dealing with death are always placed on the east and north walls, below which the dead were buried. Scenes dealing with birth occupy the opposite west wall and bulls are found only on the north wall facing the Taurus Mountains, perhaps not a coincidence. Animal heads associated with red painted niches are always on the east wall but goddesses and bull and ram heads have no special place and may occur on any wall. It is, however, rare for the south wall (the kitchen end of the shrine) to be decorated, although there are a few cases where this happened.

Fig. 17

In the earliest shrine decorated with plaster reliefs (X.1), two large bull's heads with enormous but clumsily moulded horns are placed on the north and east wall. The first is fixed on a wooden post and flanked by a doorway and a shallow niche whereas the second has its face painted red. Immediately above it are two small (rams'?) heads and towards the north-east corner there are two smaller bulls' heads without prominent horns. On the southernmost panel of the east wall there is another bull's head with shorter horns and a small head, possibly a ram's with a niche above it. Although this earliest shrine already foreshadows the much more monumental ones of Levels

17 Reconstruction of the earliest shrine in Level X (X.1)

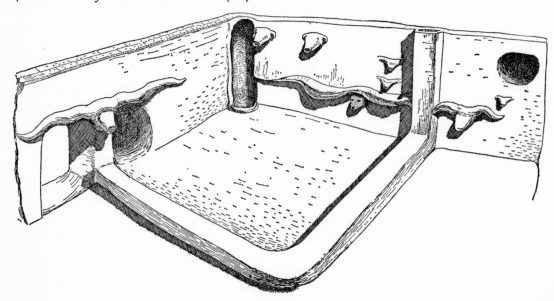

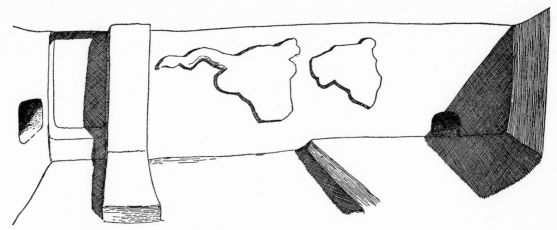

18 North wall of shrine IX.8 with animal heads cut in plaster

VII and VI, the execution of the work is still somewhat clumsy and the system of panelling is still undeveloped. This single shrine should not be taken as typical of the period, for even in Level VII, we have another (VII.35) which closely resembles it in workmanship. Shrine IX.8, next in chronological order shows the earliest example of animal heads, a feline, probably a leopard and a bull, which has lost one horn, cut deep into the plaster of the north wall, thus partly destroying the earlier painting of a large black bull. There are no traces of paint on either of these two animal-heads. A second shrine (IX.1) had a panel on the west wall with a large bull's head on the right and a smaller (ram's?) head on the left as well as wall-paintings. This building shows well developed panelling and was one of the few that had a red painted platform and a small hearth sunk in it.

Fig. 21

Fig. 18

Plate 11

Shrines of Level VII

In the restricted area in which the buildings of Level VIII were excavated no shrines with plaster reliefs were found, but painting was well established. In Level VII, however, plaster reliefs were found in not less than ten shrines. A small shrine (VII.9) had both its long walls covered with animal heads, fixed to wooden posts or to the wall in between. Three bulls' heads were placed on the east wall

Figs 19, 20

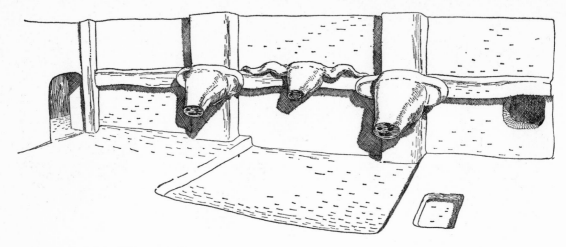

19 *East wall of shrine VII.9, restored*

Fig. 21

Fig. 15

along the line of a horizontal wooden beam whilst a fine bull's head with upturned horns graced the central panel of the west wall between two vertical posts. On the northern wall a single head with two pairs of wavy horns was fixed and the southern posts bore three superimposed heads, each with a pair of curling horns. It seems most likely that these are bulls' heads in spite of the curving horns which might at first sight suggest the horns of rams. Parallels with later representations of bull's heads on other west walls, the excessive length of the horns and the small curving horns of the actual rams found at Çatal Hüyük favour this view.

Much smaller bulls' heads are found in shrine VII.35. As in the buildings previously described, the horns are modelled in clay, but actual ram's horns are introduced into a small head on the east wall. One large bull's head spans the main panel of the north wall; two small ones are found beside it on the same wall and a larger bull's head appears below a red painted niche on the east wall. Next to this niche a pair of woman's breasts appear above the animal's right horn and a second pair, placed vertically, appear above the ram's head. From the open nipples protruded the teeth of a fox and a weasel's skull respectively which were incorporated in this pair of breasts. The east wall of shrine VII.21 combines the same symbolism, but on a much grander scale. A large ram's head with actual horns and painted with a fine meander pattern is placed beneath a bold clay

20 *West wall of shrine VII.9, restored*

horn from which a single breast protrudes. Out of the open breast springs the lower jaw of a gigantic boar with formidable tusks and its position is similar to that in shrine VII.35. The central panel of this shrine is dominated by a large bull's head with actual horns surmounting a red-painted niche and a row of six stylized breasts. Asymmetrically surrounding the bull's head are three small ram's heads with actual horns. A further breast, but with open nipple, occurs on the northernmost panel of the east wall and another is found on the

21 *North and east walls of shrine VII.35, restored*

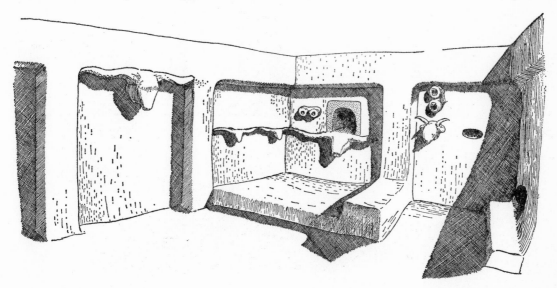

Fig. 14

opposite wall. The main feature of the west wall, however, is a huge bull's head with moulded nostrils and mouth set in a red-painted muzzle. A geometric pattern is painted on the head, the ears are red and red bands surround the horns, which are of gigantic size. Though fallen and crushed by crumbling masonry, one of the horn cores could still be measured and was over a metre in length. A niche for libations, semi-circular in shape, was set into the west wall and was matched to the right by a grooved and painted panel (in white, black and red) representing a kilim (a thin woven rug). The north wall of this building was decorated with a similar panel and with wall-paintings of vultures attacking headless corpses. A doorway, placed well above the level of the floor interrupted the wall-paintings and there may have been some short wooden steps. It was in this building that the series of human skulls, already referred to (p. 84), were found, and, with its splendid and impressive decoration, it is evidently one of the major shrines of Level VII.

Fig. 22

Hardly less remarkable is a series of three shrines (VII.10.8 and 1) that lie in a row a little farther south. The first of these (VII.10) is decorated only with plaster reliefs, and, unlike the other two, had no wall-paintings. At the bottom of the central post along the north

22 *North and east walls of shrine VII.10, restored. See Plates 10, 17*

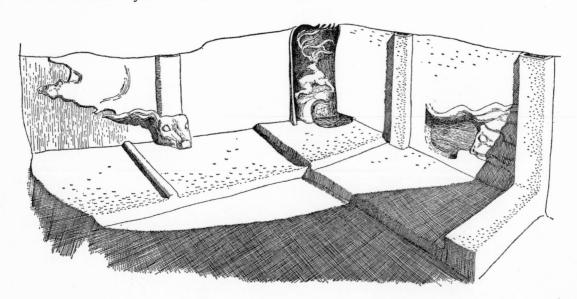

23 Reconstruction of the west and south walls of shrine VII.1 with plaster reliefs of twin goddesses and bulls' heads

wall was placed a large animal head with a single and rather short plaster horn. The plaster to the right was well preserved, so that it could be established that an animal with only one horn was portrayed. The face was demolished, but a comparison with the building immediately above (in Level VI B) where the post ended in a well preserved ram's head with two pairs of horns, may suggest that here also a ram was represented. To the left (west) of this ram's head the plaster was cut into an animal silhouette to which a little modelling of the head was added. Unfortunately the upper part was broken, but what remains suggests the outline of a stag's head. In the northeast corner a much better preserved representation of a stag on a rock was found. Here also touches of modelling were added to the cut-out silhouette of the animal, which is extremely lively and naturalistically observed. The motif of a stag turning its head appears here for the first time, but is again found in the paintings of deer-hunts in the shrine of Level III and in the pottery figure of a doe from

Plate 10

Plate 17

Plates 55, 61

109

a house in Hacılar VI. Stags are comparatively rare in the art of Çatal Hüyük, but a fine antler of Red Deer (*Cervus elaphus*) incorporated into a plaster animal head decorated the north wall of a probable shrine (VI.B.5).

The east wall of shrine VII.10 showed another cut-out relief; a vast bull's head, seen like most of the animals in this building, in profile. In front of the head is a shallow niche and the boldly curving horn, the eye and a few other features are enhanced by modelling in plaster. The reconstruction drawing shows these animals as they probably were originally, but as the result of a rough brick fill and the superimposed weight of another burnt shrine (VI.10) they have been somewhat flattened out.

Fig. 23

Very similar to the large bull's head in shrine VII.10 is a huge bull on the west and south wall of shrine VII.1. The entire outline of the animal's back and head is carved in the plaster, but the feet and belly are not indicated. The silhouette of the head is again obtained by cutting a shallow niche in front of it and the eye and horn are modelled in plaster. The head of the animal has been pressed down considerably so that the figure looks disjointed, for the entire south wall has been compressed by the weight of later buildings. The bull turns its back to another smaller horned animal, possibly a cow, which occupies the other side of the west wall and was made in the same technique. It too has no legs and seems to stand on a red-painted pedestal. When first found the figure still bore traces of an overall blue paint, and this is the only case of the use of blue paint on walls so far. Between these two animals a battered bull's head was placed below the remains of a small goddess figure, of which only the right arm, leg and breast were preserved, but the outline of the remainder of the body could still be partly traced on the plaster. The asymmetrical position of this figure was puzzling at first until it was realized that two such figures would make a balanced composition. At the point where the second figure should have been the plaster had been stripped off the wall, probably at the time when the building was condemned and filled in. Had there been only a single figure, then there is no reason for the plain plaster not to have survived, as it has done in every other building. Twin goddess figures

24 Reconstruction of the north and east walls of shrine VII.1 with wall-paintings of textiles

are by no means rare and in at least two other neighbouring shrines (VII.8 and VI.B.12) the existence of such a group is either certain or highly probable. The east and north wall of this shrine were ornamented with textile patterns but on either side of the main post plaster reliefs of breast and horn were found.

Fig. 24

Between the two shrines just described there lay another (VII.8). Its earliest decoration consisted of one enormous panel of vultures 1·8 metres high and extending over the greater part of the north and the entire east wall. At the end of its existence, after a hundred layers of white plaster had almost obliterated the existence of the vulture painting, a fine bull was cut into the thick plaster of the north wall, and painted black. As found its head was unfortunately missing, but it is seen advancing towards the doorway leading to the entrance corridor. Red-painted panels are found below the bull over two platforms on the edge of which once stood a big bucranium, the earliest of its type. More red panels continued beyond the doorway the jambs of which at one stage were gaily painted with rosettes.

Plate 12

Fig. 25

Above the red panels there were paintings with hands and in the middle of the west wall there lay again as in shrines VII.1 and VI.B.8 (immediately above it) a stylized bull's head. What particularly attracted our attention was the strange way in which the plaster of the wall had been cut, late in the life-span of the shrine. Symmetrically placed above the bull's head were the rough outlines of two felines, presumably leopards, face to face. Like the cow in shrine VII.1 next door, these stood on pedestals and directly above them all the plaster had been broken off the wall, as if something had been removed when the shrine was abandoned and filled in. That a relationship existed between the plaster reliefs in shrine VII.1 and the potentially domesticable bull and cow and the wild leopards in its neighbour soon became evident. Moreover, something had been removed from the west wall in both buildings and a comparison with a group of old and broken statuettes in blue and brown limestone, found in shrine VI.A.10, which showed two goddesses standing behind leopards and a boy riding a leopard displayed the

25 North and east walls of shrine VII.8 as found. See Plates 12, 36

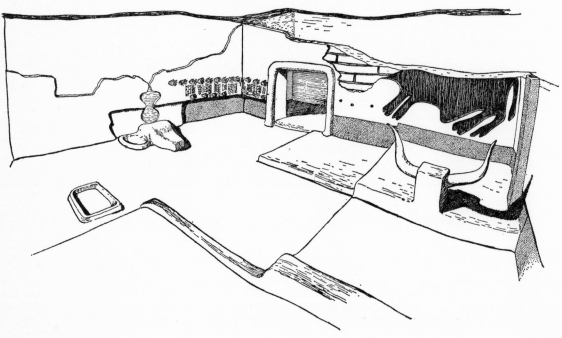

Fig. 26

26 *Restoration of the north and east walls of shrine VII.8 See Plates 12, 36*

same outline of the wild animals as found in the shrine. It is therefore quite probable that twin goddesses, like those found in shrine VII.1, were originally placed on this west wall, as is shown in the reconstruction drawing. It is moreover likely that the stone statuettes were originally part of the cult images of this shrine, from which they, like the plaster reliefs, were removed when the building was abandoned.

The next shrine of Level VII (VII.23) was relatively simple, but contained a very fine painted plaster relief of a pregnant goddess, placed on the east wall. In the later phases the goddess was painted white, but on one of the numerous white layers the small red hand of a child was painted on the goddess's breast. In her original form she had been clothed in a gaudily painted dress with patterns in red, black and orange and the dress extended like a veil behind her between the upturned arms and legs. She was shown as clearly pregnant and her condition was emphasized by the use of concentric

Plate VII

red circles. Face, hands and feet had been broken when the shrine was deserted and filled in. No other plaster reliefs or wall-paintings other than red panels marred the simple serenity of this shrine dedicated to the goddess.

Shrine VII.29 had two bulls' heads, with red-painted ears on the east wall and a red-painted niche next to the larger lower head.

Shrine VII.45 was abandoned and filled in with broken brick and plaster after its west wall had collapsed. In the middle of the north wall, set between two red-painted posts and above a red panel, sat the

Plate 25; *Fig. 27*

large figure of a goddess of which only the lower portion had survived. Below many layers of white plaster there were red vertical stripes on the legs, which show that this figure also once had a painted dress. The position of the goddess, framed by posts, gives her the appearance of coming through a door to show herself to the worshippers. The large panel on her left was plain and no traces of decoration survive on the greater part of the east wall, which, fairly late in the occupation of the shrine, was cut into the silhouette of

Plate 13

a gigantic boar's head. This is very similar to the boar figures of clay which have been found in Level VI B. A scar on the plaster nearest the central post may suggest a plastically rendered horn; another, surrounded by a circle of red paint, the presence of a small animal head. This is one of the shrines where the bench was painted red.

Plate 24

Shrine VII.31 was one of the best preserved buildings on the site even though it had lost the plaster of its entire north and more than half of the east wall. It had been abandoned and filled in after its reliefs had been defaced. Nevertheless it stood to a height of 2 metres, with one of the capitals of the wooden posts preserved

Fig. 28

intact. On entering the shrine through a doorway in the north wall one faced not less than four panels decorated with reliefs; two on the west wall, one on the south wall (the second panel was occupied by the wooden ladder) and one more on the southernmost panel of the east wall. The central panel on this wall, which frequently bears important reliefs, was destroyed down to the lowermost red panel. The first composition consisted of the familiar goddess-figure modelled in bold relief, the hands and feet of which appear to have

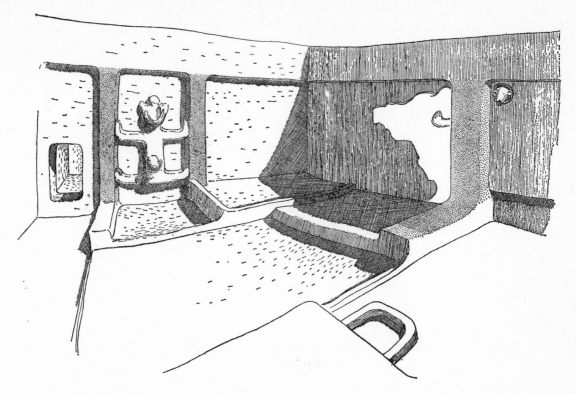

27 *Restoration of the north and east walls of shrine VII.45 with reliefs*

Fig. 28

been made separately and inserted into now empty sockets. As is normal at Çatal Hüyük, there is no indication of sex, but the navel was always shown. Above the head two holes in the plaster on either side of a slight knob indicate perhaps the former existence of a head-dress or, equally possible, they were used to fix a hanging over the sacred figure of the divinity. Above her left hand a small bull's head is shown, the ears of which had been painted red. The head also was defaced. Near her right hand the horn of a bull modelled in clay is seen and this is matched by a second on the other side of the central post, which had been removed. Evidently these belong to a bull's head modelled on the post, as in so many shrines of Level VII. The second panel was filled with five bull's heads of varying sizes, all smashed when the building was deserted, but easily recognizable from horns and scars. Beyond the corner post another figure of a goddess was placed next to a horizontal bar and below her is a shallow

Fig. 28

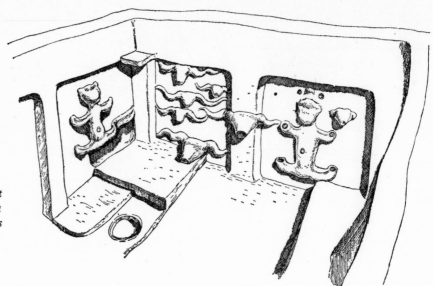

28 West and south-west walls of shrine VII.31 with the animal heads restored. See Plate 24

niche. She also had lost her head, but the entire outline is preserved which suggests a hair-style with two small horns, very like that fashionable in the fourteenth century AD. There were faded traces of paint on this figure, especially round the neck, which suggests a painted garment, but too little plaster survived to reconstruct its pattern. No traces of paint were found on the first figure, nor on the third and most remarkable one on the east wall. This goddess is

Fig. 29

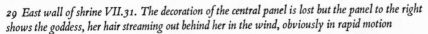

29 East wall of shrine VII.31. The decoration of the central panel is lost but the panel to the right shows the goddess, her hair streaming out behind her in the wind, obviously in rapid motion

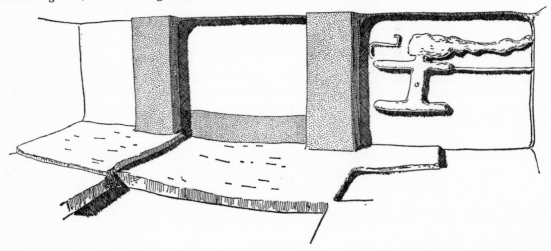

shown with her head and body in profile, her long locks floating behind her in the wind. Arms and legs are outstretched and fore-shortened, thus strengthening the impression of swift motion. The goddess appears to be running, dancing or whirling and above her right arm there originally was something, now broken, outlined in orange red paint. The destruction of the central panel may have deprived us of the object or figure to which she is seen advancing. Perhaps the clue to this lies in the building underneath. This will be explored when the excavations are resumed.

Shrines of Levels VI B and VI A

The traditional use of plaster reliefs in shrines, already fully developed in Level VII, reached its climax in Levels VI B and VI A, when we find truly monumental compositions up to 4 metres in height (shrine VI.B.10).

Fig. 38

A number of shrines of Level VI B are very simple in their decoration. Shrine VI.B.12 bore reliefs of the twin goddess on its north wall and a third (animal head?) above the main platform. Shrine VI.B.15 had two bull's heads on the south wall, one set in a recess, the other in a side room, whilst wall-paintings decorated the space above the main platform. Shrine VI.B.20 had a goddess on the south wall, but only the scar of attachment was preserved. A stag's head and a wall-painting of textile design formed the only decoration of shrine VI.B.5; a horn and breast (?) and numerous superimposed wall-paintings that of shrine VI.B.1, unless the destroyed west wall had been originally decorated with one or more goddesses like all its neighbours. Shrine VI.B.7, which has also lost its west wall, had a large goddess with horizontal arms and no legs, but from the lower part of her body projected a huge red painted bull's head similar to the Twin Goddess in shrine VI.B.14 with which it was connected through a single entrance-shaft, thus forming a double shrine. Goddess and bull's head suffered severe damage in a fire at the end of Level VI B and were covered by a new wall in Level VI A.

In the northern part of the excavated area there were two splendid shrines VI B and A.61; and VI B and A.44. The first is one of

30 East and south walls of shrine VI.61 with bucrania and horn cores set in a bench

Plates 15, 16; *Fig. 30* the largest found and presented a terrific spectacle of bucrania; two placed on the male corner-platform and a third beyond a carefully modelled bench from which six sets of aurochs horn-cores projected with a seventh raised at the end like a bucranium. The impression left by these remains is still that of tremendous male power and it may be surmised that this was a shrine devoted to the cult of the male deity. The east wall was preserved only up to a red painted groove, which marks the line of a horizontal wooden beam. It seems unlikely that the central panels would have been left plain and one would expect at least one large bull's head there (as in shrines VI.B.10 and 14). The other walls are much better preserved but bore no reliefs or wall-paintings. Like many other shrines of Level VI B it remained in use during the next period at the end of which it was burnt.

Near to this shrine was another (VI.44), built in Level VI B and occupied throughout this level and the next. Whereas in many buildings the goddess is shown in person, her presence is here ex-
Plates 18, 20; *Fig. 31* pressed in a life-size plaster relief of her attributes, a pair of leopards. These decorate the main panel on the north wall framed by two wooden plastered posts with numerous phases of painting, plain red or white or with a textile design in grey, cream and red. The leopards are placed on the middle panel above a plain red panel

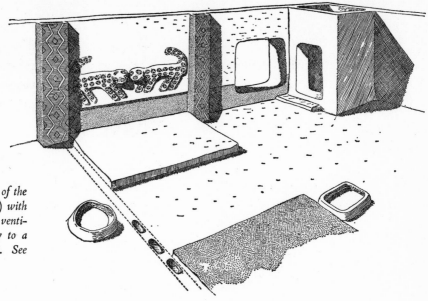

31 *North and east walls of the Leopard Shrine (VI.B.44) with a screen to the left, and a venti-lation shaft and doorway to a storeroom on the right. See Plates 18–21*

and they are each about a metre long. They face each other with raised tails; a short fat female on the left, a more slender male on the right. In the latest phases these were whitewashed and bore no designs and they were rather clumsy in shape as the result of repeated replastering. When the layers of white plaster were stripped off one by one the animals regained their original shape and painted decoration began to appear, which had been repeated over and over again. The later phases of painting showed lemon-coloured animals covered with black spots, and the line of the claws and the end of the tail, as well as the mouth, were accentuated by pink stripes. The animals were outlined by black dashes. There were a great many layers of this sort of decoration, all more or less partially preserved and affected by the fire which had consumed this building. On one of the tails, broken by a deep Hellenistic pit, an earlier form of painting could be seen and the leopards were cleaned down to the best preserved layer. They changed their spots into what looked like black rosettes placed in rows on the white bodies, legs and tails, and two rosettes formed their eyes. The mouth was red, claws and the tip of the tail being outlined in bright red paint. This form of decoration was also repeated at least twenty times and the fine three- or four-petalled rosettes are indeed a very close rendering of actual spots on leopards. The left-hand leopard, badly cracked and weakened by the

Plates 20, 21

Plates 18, 19, VI

119

water that had seeped into the Hellenistic pit, broke upon removal and we were thus able to remove some more layers of paint. This showed that the earliest leopards were considerably smaller and had black claws and their rosettes were much larger and fewer than in the later paintings. There appear to have been about forty layers of painting on them.

The leopards have now been reconstituted in the Ankara Archaeological Museum. On the edge of the platform in front of the leopards a red-painted bull's head was found crushed in its fall. It cannot have fallen from the south wall which was preserved and showed no scars of attachment, nor is it likely that it had been fixed on the screen of sticks and plaster which divided the kitchen end of the shrine from the main room. One can only surmize that it could have been placed in the middle of the north wall, well above the leopards, but this is by no means certain. There were also the remains of a bucranium, but again in the absence of any mark of attachment on the platform,

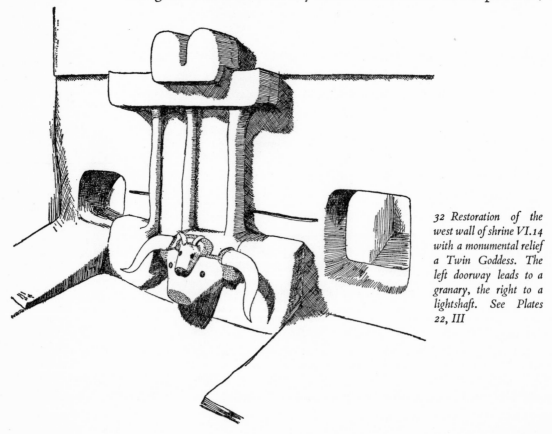

32 Restoration of the west wall of shrine VI.14 with a monumental relief a Twin Goddess. The left doorway leads to a granary, the right to a lightshaft. See Plates 22, III

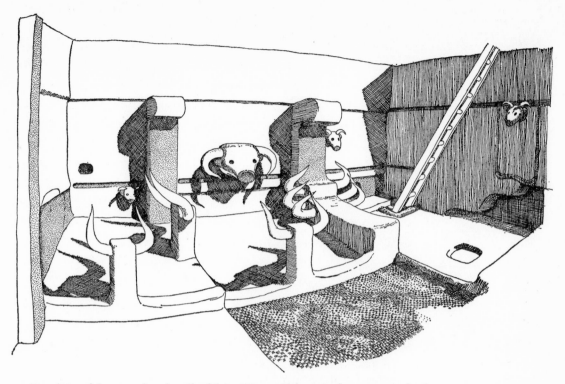

33 Restoration of the east and south walls of shrine VI.14 with bucrania, horn cores on a bench and bulls' and rams' heads modelled in relief. A ladder, the normal means of entry, is on the right

its original position is uncertain, and may only appear when the platform is stripped of its plaster. A rich collection of stone statuettes, grain offerings and stalactites was found in this room (see pp. 202–3).

The well preserved shrine VI.B and A.14, the eastern member of a twin shrine (14 and 7), offers certain analogies to shrine VI.61 in having three bucrania and a bench with three sets of horn cores, the easternmost of which is likewise raised above the others. Three animal heads with actual horns were found on the east wall; a large bull's head above the horizontal beam and two rams' heads set at different heights on the flanking panels. Another was set within a frame on the south wall beyond the ladder and above a deep recess, with a sinuous outline reminiscent of the horns of bulls in plaster reliefs of Level VII. It is, however, the west wall which bore a strange and monumental relief, 2·2 metres in height and therefore among the largest yet found at Çatal Hüyük. Although damaged by fire and partly collapsed it can be restored on paper as a stylized twin

Figs 32, 33
Plate III

Figs 22, 23

figure of a goddess with two heads and bodies, but with a single pair of arms and upturned legs. The bodies were modelled on two vertical wooden posts and the plaster edges were painted red. From the abdomen of the right-hand body an enormous bull's head, nearly 61 cms in width, with powerful horns protruded. On top of it a smaller head was modelled. Not less than a hundred layers of plaster covered the heads, out of which at least six or seven were painted. In the latest phase (VI.A) the muzzles have lost their nostrils and mouth and the painting is confined to a red muzzle, red ears and rings round the horns. In the earlier layers a hand placed over the mouth is painted with the fingers spread out over the animal's nose. In these twin shrines the same subject is represented; the birth of the bull god from the body of the goddess, but whereas in shrine VI.B.7 there is only one goddess, here are two of which only one is giving birth. The shoulder and part of one head were found crushed in the debris of the shrine (the other shoulder had lost the second head), but it appears that the head was flat and if any features were shown they must have been executed in paint. The heads may have been very similar to those of the contemporary white marble statuette of a twin goddess found in shrine VI.A.10.

A row of three bull's heads, separated by small knobs (stylized breasts?) and one ram's head, all richly painted, decorated the central and south panels of the east wall of shrine VI.B.8. Many of the patterns found on these heads (thirteen layers of paint were recorded) are identical with those on the bulls' heads in shrine VI.14. Here also three sets of horn cores were set into the bench, with the eastern-most raised above the others. The main decoration of the east wall consisted of several layers of fine wall-paintings (see p. 162) but the most striking feature of the room was a great bull sunk in the plaster of the north wall. This was replastered over and over again and was sometimes red, sometimes white. It occupied exactly the same position as its predecessor, the black bull in shrine VII.8, which lies immediately below this building. The continuity in cult, so characteristic of Çatal Hüyük, could hardly be illustrated better. A black bull occurred on the north wall in Level IX, vultures in Levels VIII and early VII; a black bull in late VII and in VI B and A; and

Plate 22

Plate 70

Plate IV; *Figs 34, 35*

Fig. 36

Plate 14

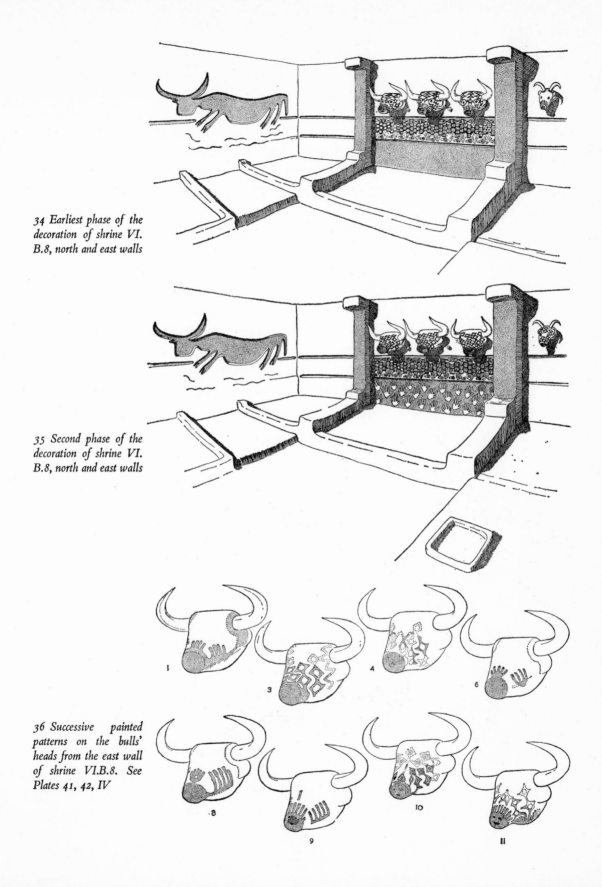

34 Earliest phase of the decoration of shrine VI. B.8, north and east walls

35 Second phase of the decoration of shrine VI. B.8, north and east walls

36 Successive painted patterns on the bulls' heads from the east wall of shrine VI.B.8. See Plates 41, 42, IV

panels of hands in VII and VI B, always in the same building. The people who made the red bull, 2·4 metres in length, may have seen the somewhat smaller black one and copied the design. The west wall of the shrine bore the familiar representation of a goddess, originally about 1·2 metres in height, with raised arms and up-turned feet, a position indicative of childbirth. Immediately below her a large bull's head with spreading horns, modelled in clay and plaster, is shown. The representation is clear and shows the goddess having given birth to a bull. One of the many layers of plaster was painted yellow, but without any traces of patterns. A second bull's head, originally painted and with aurochs horns lay crushed at the foot of the wall from which it must have fallen.

Plate 26; *Fig. 37*

One more shrine (VI.B.10) of this building-level remains to be described. Of this the north wall was still standing to its original

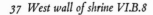

37 West wall of shrine VI.B.8

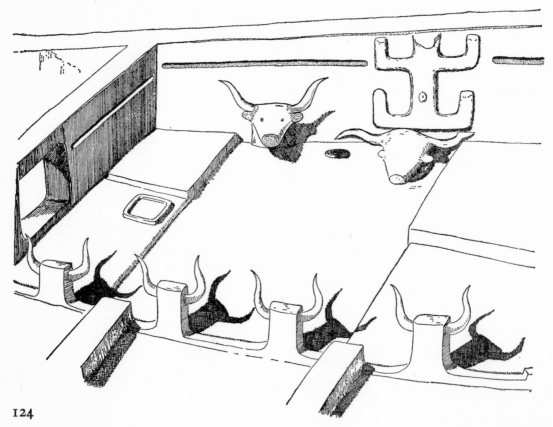

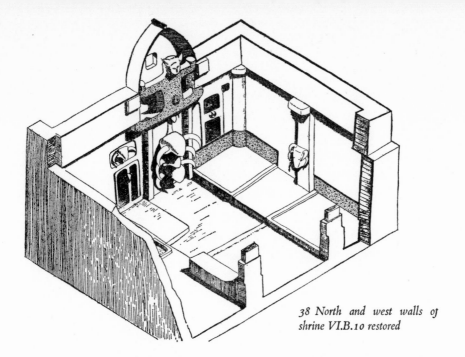

38 *North and west walls of shrine VI.B.10 restored*

height of 3·35 metres. It continued in use during Level VI A, during which the floor-level rose 60 cms, but even this height was insufficient to take the monumental plaster panel on the west wall, about 30 cms higher than the ceiling, so that the central part of the building must have been raised, probably in the form of a berceau made of reeds and plaster or constructed in wood as in the Lycian houses.

Fig. 38

A large figure of a goddess, of which only the legs and part of the body remained *in situ*, was shown in the position of giving birth to a ram (shown as a ram's head in the customary manner). The scene is supported by a frame which contains three superimposed heads of bulls with aurochs horns. In one of the many phases of decoration, the figure of the goddess was painted yellow, as the one in shrine VI.8. On either side of the frame there were deep niches in the wall; between the two at the left hand side of the goddess a lower jaw of a boar was inserted into the wall and the frame round the niches was painted with checkerboard patterns. The high deep niche on the other side was subdivided by a vertical partition on which was fixed a ram's head, and a small bull's head surmounted this in a shallow recess. A large ram's head with two pairs of actual horns was placed on the central post along the north wall, and a large bull's head appeared from the east wall above a deep, red-painted niche. In

Plate 28; *Fig. 39*

Level VI B poorly preserved wall-paintings surrounded this head, which may also have been painted, but as the result of the conflagration it was far too difficult to clean. Between the bull's head and the post a pair of pendulous woman's breasts appeared, open at the nipple end and painted red like the muzzle of the bull. From each of them the beak of a Griffon Vulture (*Gyps vulvus*) protruded, as each breast contained a complete skull. Beyond the post a horn was moulded in plaster and, as in shrine VII.23, the only entrance into the building lay through a doorway set high up in the wall. The panel below it was painted in the VI B period.

During its occupation in Level VI A, the floor level of the shrine rose by 60 cms and the animal heads gradually sank to floor-level; a bucranium was erected on the corner platform and the wall-paintings on the east and west walls were covered with white plaster. A new façade was built in front of the niches on either side of the main plaster panel on the west wall, which remained unaltered until it was destroyed by fire at the end of Level VI A.

Fig. 40

39 North and east walls of shrine VI.B.10 with entrance on the right

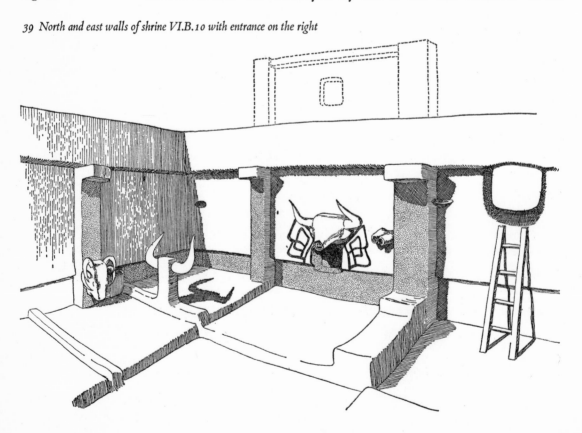

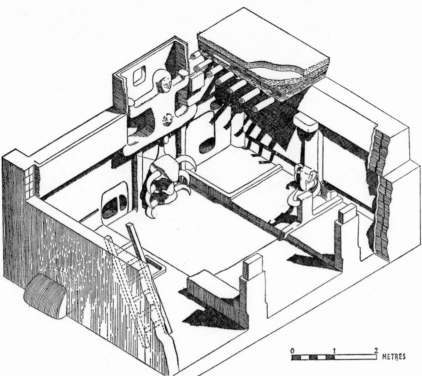

40 North and west walls of shrine VI.A.10 restored

The destruction of this building preserved a fine collection of stone statuettes *in situ* on the floor, for with the stone tools at their disposal the inhabitants of Çatal Hüyük were unable to dig them out from under the thick layers of burnt brick fused together by the tremendous heat of the fire.

As in this shrine, the wall-paintings of shrine VI.B.8 were covered with plaster during the new period (VI.A) and two plaster beams, an upper red one, and a lower white one, were laid over the old paintings. In these 'beams' the lower jaws of boar were inserted, nine in the upper and four in the lower. The bulls' and the single ram's head remained in use and were repainted and two additional small bulls' heads were placed on the northernmost panel of the east wall. Four bucrania were erected in a row on the edges of the platforms and the sunk bull relief was replastered like the entire west wall. The horns in the bench were abolished. After a fire in which the tusks of the

Plate 27; *Fig. 41*

127

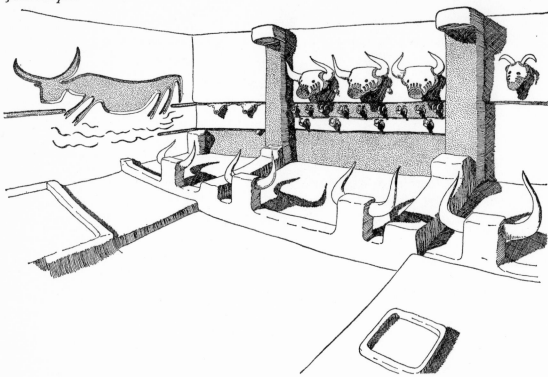

41, 42 *Decoration of the north and east walls of shrine VI.A.8. Above the third phase, and below the fourth phase. See Plate 27*

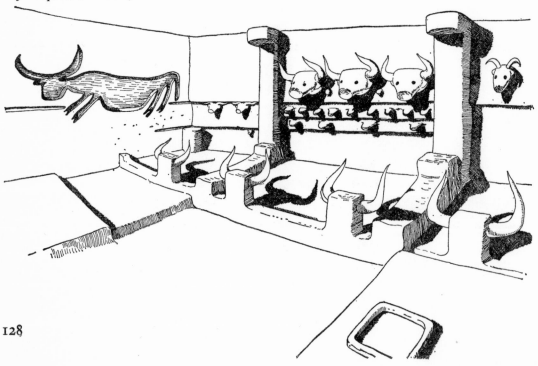

boars got burnt, the entire building was replastered and each boar's jaw was turned into a woman's breast. In this last phase of the occupation of this shrine, there were no wall-paintings and when the building was deserted its doorway was bricked up and the room filled with earth and unburnt brick.

Fig. 42

The burnt shrine VI.B.7 was remodelled in VI.A and a new east wall was inserted in front of the old one. Its new doorway was raised above floor-level and a red-painted niche was set in the main panel of the wall. A fine ram's head and a bull's head (both with actual horns) were placed on either side of the southern post, and both heads were painted with human hands. On the edge of the platform a 'bucranium' was set up, incorporating not the horns of a bull, but those of a big ram.

Plate V; *Fig. 43*

No actual changes seem to have been made during period VI.A in shrines VI.16, 61 and 44, except continual repaintings. Shrines VI.B.29 and 31 were built above their Level VII predecessors. The former building may still have been a shrine and like VI.A.30 may have had a relief along its west wall, for which there are certain indications. Shrine VI.B and A.31 was built on top of shrine VII.31 but except for two fine bulls' heads, framed by plastered posts nothing has survived of the decoration of this room, even the plaster was stripped off the walls. Other shrines of Level VI.B, such as 12, 1 and 5, seem to have been turned into houses and 15 and 29

Plate 23

43 East wall of shrine VI.A.7 with doorway on the left. See Plate V

were filled in to form a courtyard. Two bulls' heads were found on the walls of shrine VI.A.25 as well as a fine group of stone statuettes and it looks as if this building took the place of shrine VI.B.15 next door. In the northern area, room VI.A.66, with a fine painted bull's head and a panel of symbols and small human figures, is probably a subsidiary shrine. Two others, VI.A.50 and 51 have horns set in the benches.

After the destruction of Level VI A, a number of shrines may have been rebuilt over the main shrines in the southern area (E.V.3, 5, 6, 8) but their remains are so denuded that one cannot be certain. Fragments of reliefs, too scanty to be described here, were found in E.V.12, 2 and 4 (bull's head with paint), buildings which were probably shrines and the successors of the Leopard Shrine, shrine VI.A.25 and VI.B.15 respectively. The fragments merely show that the practice of decorating sanctuaries with plaster reliefs survived into Level V, but none of a later date have been found.

Before discussing the religion of the people of Çatal Hüyük, the development of wall-painting, the other technique of shrine- and house-decoration must claim our attention.

VII

Wall-paintings

PAINTING WAS PRACTISED at Çatal Hüyük throughout the life of the settlement; the earliest fragments of wall-painting come from the building rubbish found below a house of Level X and the latest covered walls in Level II, by which period paint was also applied to light-coloured pots, though not yet on any scale. Painting was not confined to walls, but was also applied to plaster reliefs, clay statuettes, skeletons, wood, baskets and finally to pottery. It may be assumed that textiles were dyed, and paint was certainly applied to eyes and eyebrows, cheeks and lips of the women, if not to their bodies. In short, the people of Çatal Hüyük painted what they could and when they could. Excavations at aceramic Hacılar, Mesolithic Beldibi and the Upper Palaeolithic caves of Oküzlü'In and Kara'In on the subtropical south coast of Anatolia have shown the earlier phases of a well-established tradition of painting in Turkey.

At Çatal Hüyük a full range of pigments was in use, derived on the whole from minerals, such as iron oxides (red, brown and yellow ochres), copper ores (bright blue azurite, green malachite), mercury oxide (cinnabar for a deep red), red, possibly from haematite, manganese mauve or purple, galena for lead grey. The plaster background is cream or dead white and was locally available from the Pleistocene lake beds. Black was obtained from soot. The colours were finely ground with pestle and mortar but not perhaps mixed with animal fat or vegetable oil or white of egg, though all of which were available, dried in lumps or shaped into crayons and spread on flat stone palettes. Fine brush strokes imply the use of brushes, some extremely fine, whereas plain panels of red may have been painted with the use of a rag dipped in a pot of paint, as is still done today in the villages around Çatal Hüyük. Once in Level VI, mica, a mineral, finely pounded was added to the mauve paint to produce a glittering effect.

The paint was applied directly to the wall without previous tracing of outlines and the painters were evidently sure enough of themselves to dispense with this preliminary procedure. In a series of unfinished paintings in shrine A.III.8 the process of execution of an elaborate textile pattern can be followed in detail (see p. 154). The recurrence of numerous patterns and the complete repainting of complicated scenes, such as a deer hunt, about four times suggests the existence of 'books' of patterns and scenes, probably on cloth or felt.

The following colours were in use: all shades of red and brown, buff and yellow, pink and orange, mauve, grey and black, and blue. All these were used in wall-painting, but blue occurs once only, though both blue and green were used for painting parts of skeletons in Levels VII, VI B and VI A. Polychrome paintings are as common as monochrome ones and are not confined to any period.

In shrines and houses, wall-paintings had a ritual function. When the painting had served its purpose—we do not know how long this took, it may have been a year or the duration of certain festivals—it was covered with a layer of white plaster. The same area might be repainted at a later date and there may be as many as a dozen paintings on one wall, but this is not common and there may be a hundred layers of white plaster covering a wall-painting. During the vast majority of the years when shrines and houses were in use their walls were white.

Wall-paintings at Çatal Hüyük may be divided into six groups:

1 Plain panels of paint without any motifs, usually red, orange, pinkish red or brownish red. Black panels occur only in shrine VII.21.

2 Panels of geometric patterns in monochrome or polychrome, simple or elaborate with repetitive motifs, rectilinear or curvilinear.

3 Panels with symbols; solid circles, quatrefoils, crenellations, stylized flowers or stars, etc.

4 Human hands, either isolated or grouped into panels or borders of hands framing panels with geometric or naturalistic designs.

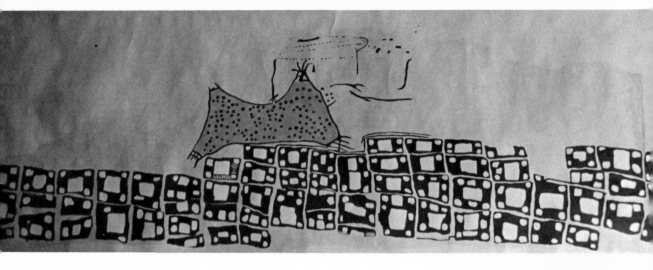

59, 60 Copy and original of a landscape painting from north and east walls of shrine VII.14. In the foreground is a town rising in graded terraces closely packed with rectangular houses. Behind the town an erupting volcano is shown, its sides covered with incandescent volcanic bombs rolling down the slope of the mountain. Others are thrown up from the erupting cone above which hovers a cloud of smoke and ashes. The twin cones suggest that an eruption of Hasan Dağ, rising to a height of 10,672 feet (3,553 metres) and standing at the eastern end of the Konya Plain and visible from Çatal Hüyük, is recorded. *See* Plate I

61–63 The Hunting Shrine of Çatal Hüyük III (A.III.1). The east wall was decorated with a long scene of dancing hunters, armed with bows and clubs and dressed in skins and bonnets of leopard skin, and a number of deer. Only the left hand fragment was *in situ*, *above*, the rest had slipped down into a Hellenistic robbers trench (visible above a woman's skull treated with red ochre, *below right*), but could be restored on paper. Among the dancers are some lively naked acrobats, a man striking

a drum and a number of strange figures, painted half red, half white which were possibly headless. A similar figure from the north wall of the shrine, beyond the big bull shown in Plate 64, is armed with a mace, *below left*. Below the floor of the shrine only female burials were found, and there were no burials below the platform normally occupied by the male of the house, a situation without parallel at Çatal Hüyük

64 An enormous red bull occupied the greater part of the north wall of shrine A.III.1, once again emphasizing the strength of religious tradition at Çatal Hüyük, where bulls always occupy this position (Plates 11, 12, 14) facing the Taurus ('Bull') Mountains, perhaps not a coincidence. This great beast, over six feet long, dominates the decoration of the shrine and the awe inspired by this monster is clearly shown by the small size of the male figures that surround it. The tops of the horns, tail and the lower part of the legs with the hoofs are lost. Between the horns stands another figure painted half white, half red and above, in front and behind are male hunters, dressed in monochrome red skins (and not leopard skins), unfortunately poorly preserved. Though some are armed and the excited hunters surround the animal, no wounding or killing is shown and it is doubtful whether the scene represents the hunt

65 This limestone concretion, from shrine VI.A.10, of which only the top was carved into a human head probably embodies the chthonic aspect of the Mother Goddess. Semi-aniconic, it emphasizes the fear and awe inspired by stalacmitic underground caverns of the Taurus Mountains, the haunt of the Earth Goddess and the realm of the dead

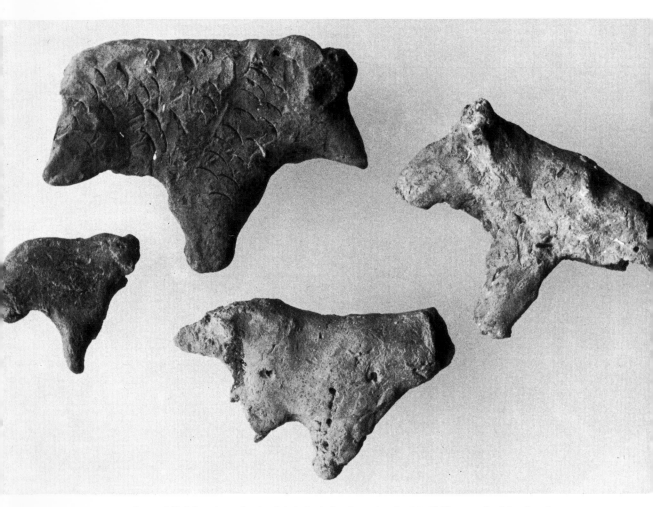

66 Coarsely modelled figurines of animals in baked clay from Level VI. Wild boar and a feline head are on the left, a horned animal (bull or cow) on the right and a headless figure below. The coarse bristles of the boar are shown by nail imprints. Nearly all these figures are intentionally maimed or broken and many bear 'wounds' inflicted with obsidian arrows or other offensive weapons. Found in groups buried in pits, these figures had evidently been used in a hunting ritual in which they had served as substitutes for the animals the hunters hoped to kill

67, 68 Large clay figure of a goddess supported by two felines, giving birth to a child. An early example of the concept of the goddess as 'Mistress of Animals', it was found in a grain bin of shrine A.II.1, where it may have been placed to promote the fertility of the crops by sympathetic magic

69 Semi-aniconic figure of a pregnant (?) goddess in blue limestone from shrine VI.A.10. It consists of a small boulder with incised eyes and mouth, sufficient to turn the stone into a shape resembling a woman. Çatal Hüyük VI has yielded examples of several theoretical stages of sculpture. They range from the aniconic but highly suggestive concretions and stalactites, purely natural and unworked by human hand, through semi-aniconic figures in which a likeness was enhanced with a few lines by the sculptor (Plates 65, 69, 72); a head or arms added to statuettes carved with a minimum of detail (Plates 70, 71, 88, 91), or fully realistic, but schematized human forms (Plates 78–80, 83–87)

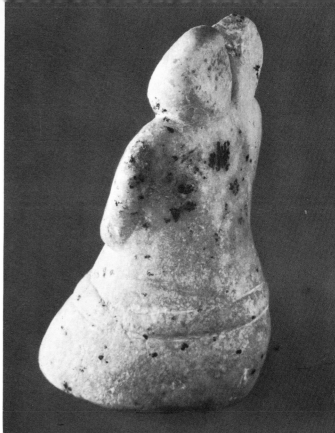

70–72 White marble figures from shrine VI.A.10: a double goddess *above*, a small schematized figure *below*. The double goddess with two heads, two pairs of breasts, but a single pair of arms is the earliest representation yet of a concept familiar to Anatolian religion, recurring later at Hacılar I and Kültepe. It probably represents the two aspects, mother and maiden, of the great goddess, predecessors of the 'Two Ladies' of the Knossos texts, the famous ivory from Mycenae and the Demeter and Kore of Classical Greece

73–76 The pair of statues of goddesses with leopards, in brown and blue lime-stone, (each shown in front and back view), were found together with a boy on a leopard (Plate 86). Evidently made by the same sculptor, they reflect the same recurrent idea of mother and maiden, here amplified by the addition of a male child. These statues were found in shrine VI.A.10, but they were already old and headless and they may originally have come from shrine VII.8. Accompanied by their sacred animal, the leopard, these statues stress the aspect of the deities as Mistress and

Master of Animals, the connection with nature and wildlife. The goddesses stand behind the animals, whereas the boy god rides on it. Of the pair, the mature nude figure, *left*, in brown limestone is evidently the mother, whereas the young figure with a shawl of skin round the neck, *right*, in blue limestone evidently represents the daughter, or maiden aspect of the goddess. The figure of the boy god is in brown limestone, like that of his mother, a subtle distinction which is typical of neolithic Çatal Hüyük

< 77 This fine alabaster figure of a standing goddess is carved in the more naturalistic style characteristic of the later building-levels of Çatal Hüyük. It was found in the storeroom of shrine E.IV.4. The burning of the building has caused the alabaster to blister which accounts for the great patch on the body of the figure and her left arm. The hole in the head is peculiar and may have served for the attachment of a cap, crown or flower? As with all these early statuettes, the figure lacks a mouth

78, 79 *Above*, the upper part of a fine marble statue with arms worked in the round and delicately carved breasts. The lower half of the figure was already lost when it was deposited in shrine VI.A.10. The fine, painted baked clay statue, *below*, was found in the anteroom of shrine VI.A.61 and shows a delicacy of modelling in hands and breasts not often encountered. The figure is painted with cross-like flower patterns, familiar from the wall-paintings. To date it is the earliest example of a naturalistically modelled figure in clay from Anatolia

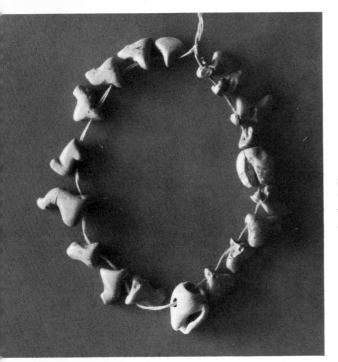

81 Necklace of blue apatite beads, graded in size, and in the shape of highly schematized steatopygous goddesses, with two shell pendants. Found with the red ochre burial of a young woman (?) below the large building IV.8. The schematic goddesses have clear links with similar figures from Peterfels in Baden and representations of women in French caves of the Upper Palaeolithic

80, 82 Kneeling figure of white marble, partly burnt, depicting a goddess from shrine VI.A.25, found together with the figure of a bird of prey, *below*, probably a vulture, and the statue of an adolescent male god (Plate 84). It is likely that the grim owl-faced deity with the vulture represents yet another aspect of the goddess; the goddess of death, the crone of later mythology

83 Unique greenish-grey schist plaque from shrine VI.A.30 with four figures in bold relief. On the left a couple of deities are shown in embrace; on the right a mother holding a child, whose head is unfortunately lost. It is possible, if not probable, that the two scenes relate a succession of events; the union of the couple on the left and the intended result on the right. The goddess remains the same, the male appears either as husband or as son. This may be one of the earliest representations of the *hieros gamos*, the 'sacred marriage'

5 Naturalistic paintings; goddesses, human figures, bulls, birds, vultures, leopards, deer found either by themselves or grouped into elaborate scenes like deer hunts, bulls with human figures, funerary rites, etc.

6 Representations of landscape and architecture; volcano and town and mortuary structures.

The distribution of these varied subjects is indicated in the table on p. 81 which indicates the range of such subjects in the various building-levels so far excavated. Subject to confirmation by later excavations it appears that groups 1 and 2 (plain and geometric panels) span almost the entire period from Level X to II and III respectively. Group 3 (symbols) also runs from Level X–III, but human hands (group 4) have not so far been found after Level VI A and group 6 is represented only in Levels VII and VI. Naturalistic paintings have a wide range, starting in Level IX with a black bull, but vultures occur only in VIII and VII and human figures are rare in the lower levels (VIII–VI A). Elaborate and lively scenes of hunting, etc., appear to be characteristic only of the end of the period in Levels IV and III, where they occur in four shrines.

A preliminary analysis then shows the existence side by side of geometric and naturalistic painting, as in the earlier Upper Palaeolithic of Europe and Anatolia. In the Early Chalcolithic painted pottery we find the continuation of both these groups, especially in the pottery of Hacılar where the geometric designs are accompanied by the 'fantastic style', which includes purely naturalistic forms with highly schematized elements of the same nature (birds, bulls, rams, snakes, etc.).

The use of red paint on panels, posts, niches, doorways and sometimes on benches, platforms or animal-heads in plaster, architectural or decorative details of houses and shrines is widespread and hardly a single well-preserved house is without it. It is obviously part of the building-tradition and it has survived in a number of villages around Çatal Hüyük to the present day. It has no structural significance and its use must therefore be regarded as ritual. It is paralleled by the red ochre burials or the use of red paint on baskets and boxes and in each case red paint, symbolic of blood and life, has a protective function. It wards off evil spirits and protects the object so decorated, be it the body of the dead, the wall of the house or shrine near which he slept, the bench or platform on which he sat or slept, the posts which support his roof and which might fall down, the boxes in which precious possessions were kept or the baskets in which his food was stored. In a world filled with evil spirits such protection was essential and if we could only discover the colour of garments we might safely assume that red cloth was made for this very purpose. There is one scrap of evidence which proves the use of red cloth; a number of broken beads in Level VI contained red stains of thread and as no red ochre was present in the grave, these can only have come from the thread. Nor is it at all impossible to assume that the red panels over the platforms imitate hangings of red cloth, just as the geometric panels copy patterned textiles. Rows of holes for fixing such hangings occur in a number of shrines (VII.8; VI.A.10) in a position at the

Figs 25, 26 foot of the wall, where such panels with imitation hangings are most often found.

It is probably not a coincidence that solid black panels have been found only below the vulture painting in shrine VII.21, where they alternate in time with red ones. In this context black evidently represents death and mourning. How far the inhabitants of Çatal Hüyük carried this symbolism is difficult to tell, but we have found black vultures and red vultures, red bodies and one faded black body (in room VI.A.27), black bulls and red bulls, and rows of alternate red hands and black hands. Such contrasts need not be purely decorative and probably have a meaning. It may be argued that red and black are some of the easiest available colours, but the paintings at Çatal Hüyük, more often polychrome than not, show no lack of pigments available so that such a theory is hardly tenable. Nor should we attach too much importance to a naturalistic rendering of colours in the depiction of humans and animals. The male population of Çatal Hüyük, though naturally sunburnt, was white skinned, but males are painted red with black hair. Women are painted red or white and, though it may be argued that they were less sun-tanned than the men, they nevertheless worked in the fields or on the roofs of the houses where they would be exposed to the sun. The white figures of women might indicate a white dress rather than white bodies and the evidence is quite inconclusive. They are distinguished from the men in shape rather than in colour. The same applies to the bulls, and, whereas the male aurochs was probably black in colour, the huge red figures in shrines VI.8 and III.1 are evidently also bulls judging by their horns and the only possible figure of a cow (shrine VII.1) was painted blue! Also vultures in life are neither red nor black but brown.

Prima facie acceptance of the colours as naturalistic would create a naïve picture of a polychrome society of red or white women, red men with red or black hands pursuing blue cows and red and black bulls, which is anything but convincing.

Panels with geometric decoration are common and varied and may also be used for the decoration of plastered posts (as in the Leopard Shrine VI.B.44 or house A.III.10), although these are usually painted red. Sometimes the patterns consist of groups of parallel vertical (house VI.B.28) or horizontal lines (house VIII.1); frequently more elaborate patterns are preferred, such as great panels of concentric circles in shrine VIII.2 above a dado of black and red triangles. On the east wall of this shrine these were repeated four times but on the north wall they only formed a single layer. L-shaped patterns in red or orange covered the main panel on the north wall of house VI.B.3 and the panel below the doorway in shrine VI.B.10. Checkerboard patterns surrounded the niche below the boar's jaw in the same building; superimposed triangles, half red, half white, a post in house A.III.10. Vertical wavy lines in red surrounded a niche painted orange in shrine III.13, horizontal ones decorate the bull's head in shrine VI.A.66; A-shaped patterns, upright and reversed in black and red, cover a panel on the west wall of house VI.B.45. Groups of orange dots occupied the lower panel of the north wall of shrine VI.A.66, the central eastern panel of which bore a pattern of concentric circles and pointed stars in white and orange on cream. Many of these are too fragmentary to reconstruct, but hardly any two are the same. Some, like the orange painting from the north wall of shrine IX.1, defy interpretation.

Plates 30, VIII;
Figs 14, 15

Fig. 24

Plates 30, VIII

Plate 29; *Fig. 44*

Another series, however, starting with a polychrome painting in shrine IX.8 and continuing with a whole group in Levels VIII–VI A, evidently represent textiles and their resemblance to Anatolian 'kilims' (*i.e.* thin woven rugs) is striking. As weaving was widely practised at Çatal Hüyük and dyeing would present no difficulties, since all the necessary plants for the production of vegetable dyes grow wild around the mound, the probability that kilims were already produced should seriously be considered. In this connection it is particularly interesting to note that two of these wall-paintings from shrine VII.21 imitate a stitched border. On a painting this makes no sense unless a kilim provided its prototype. In two superimposed wall-paintings from shrine VII.1 the stitched border, indicated by impression in the previous shrine, is painted as a row of light and dark squares, neatly marking the edge of the kilim. Rather than suggesting that these wall-paintings inspired the later weaving of kilims, these borders indicate the reverse, and it seems now likely that kilims have been woven in Anatolia since the late seventh millennium BC, or for at least the last eight thousand years.

Favourite motifs of these kilim patterns are rectangles filled with Union Jack patterns, alternate rows of red and black triangles with a central white dot, or squares filled with concentric lozenges, with or without a border. This may be grooved (as in shrine VII.21) or merely painted (shrines VII.1 and 8, and VI.B.1 or VI.A.50), but in a number of cases it was faint and could not be preserved (*e.g.* shrines VI.B.15, IX.8 and VIII.8).

Whereas the kilim patterns of Levels IX–VII are fairly simple, those of Levels VI B and VI A show great sophistication and a new motif is introduced which looks like a string of vertically or diagonally arranged lozenges, varying in shape and size and combined with zigzag and wavy lines. Other elements look like the fine mesh of a shawl or a pattern of bricks or openwork reed matting, but their origin is probably to be sought in the sophisticated textiles of this period. About a dozen such paintings covered the two panels of the east wall of shrine VI.B.1, which was repainted over and over again. Continuity in decoration marks this building which was built on top of an earlier shrine in Level VII similarly decorated with numerous

44 North and east wall of shrine VI.B.1 with the 'mortuary' wall-painting on the north wall, and textiles and kilim pattern paintings over the main platforms. On the wall beyond the bench are painted 'bones'. See Plates 8, 29

kilim-patterns. Many of these paintings were exceedingly fragmentary and the conflagration which destroyed this building twice in Level VI has reduced the fine layers of plaster to the thickness of a dead leaf as well as changing its colour. The earliest of the textile paintings is also one of the most complicated; many of the later paintings on the northern panel resemble each other without being identical. The finest of all, one of the latest, though only half preserved and measuring nearly 1·8 metres in length, has a pattern as complicated as many a modern kilim and is painted in red, white, orange-red and grey on buff. Not only the general effect, but the colour variations in the vertical bands, without affecting the pattern, is that of a textile. Within the triangles the fill motif resembles a stylized flower or, less likely, a four-fingered hand. The central vertical bands show a simplified design whereas the broader outer bands are more elaborate. There is some evidence to show that this kilim pattern was once repainted, but not enough survived to be certain that the later painting followed exactly the same pattern. Along the top a border with a wavy line on alternate red and white background marked the kilim's edge below a plastered horizontal beam. Fragments of a similar kilim pattern, also with red and white mesh bordering a triangle were found in house VI.B.3 next door, and another version is seen on the posts of the Leopard Shrine.

Plate 29; *Fig. 44*

Fig. 29

153

Plates 37, 38; *Fig. 45*

Kilim patterns of the same sort decorated the east and north walls of the somewhat later shrine VI.A.50. Of these the one on the main panel of the east wall, was the most interesting and was painted in red, black and white. Against a mesh background three vertical bands of lozenges with rounded triangles on either side stand out. The fill-motifs are more varied here; stylized flowers, crosses, horns and even a small hand. The other paintings lack the mesh background, and the semicircles have no fill-motifs.

Simpler textile patterns consisting of vertical bands with zigzag or lozenge motifs occurred in shrines VI.B.1 and VI.B.15, and a particularly interesting pattern in red was found in house VI.B.65.

Plate 35

Panels with 'leopard spots', identical with the patterns on the leopard reliefs are less common, but they occurred in the richly painted shrine VI.B.1. It is possible that these paintings replaced actual hangings of leopard skin, in the same way as red panels and kilim paintings replaced actual cloth and textiles.

In Levels V and IV only fragments of striped patterns and two triangles painted in black were found on the central post of the east wall of shrine E.IV.1. In Level III, however, an entire shrine (A.III.8) was ornamented with kilim and textile patterns. The latest of these is unfinished, but was meant to cover the entire building except the south wall, as is clear from the red triangles covering all three walls.

Plates 31, 32

In fact, only the painting of the north-west corner was completed. Two rows of vertical panels divided by parallel horizontal lines formed the pattern and each panel contained groups of lines diagonally arranged in a zigzag pattern rather like woven mats. The triangular interstices were filled with red paint. From the unfinished panels the painter's method can be followed in detail: first he put down the red triangles, leaving space enough for the white ones; then he put in the grey ground in stripes, leaving white lines round the red triangles and thirdly and finally he repainted the white lines. This final over-painting in white was clearly to be seen in the most perfect areas of the painting. Some pleasant irregularities in the design are similar to deliberate 'faults' in Anatolian kilims, the idea being that perfect work can only be made by God. The way in which this kilim was intended to cover the walls—running round the

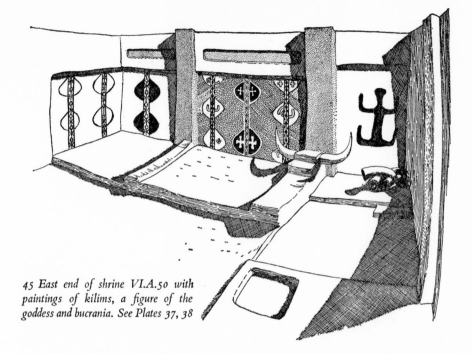

45 East end of shrine VI.A.50 with paintings of kilims, a figure of the goddess and bucrania. See Plates 37, 38

corners of the room—gives one the sense of a wall-hanging of enormous size (14·4 metres, or over 45 feet).

Below this painting on part of the west wall was another consisting of two vertical rows of red crosses or flowers outlined in pink and associated with crenellations of an even earlier layer with quatrefoils in orange-red with a pink border. Elements of this earliest pattern have also survived on the north and east wall, associated with barbed zigzag lines (honeycombs in section ?) and other motifs. These may be regarded as textile motifs and at the same time as symbols, presumably of fertility. A pattern of deep red dots and V's, it would seem, immediately preceded the unfinished kilim pattern, so that there is evidence for not less than four superimposed patterns on the west wall (orange-red quatrefoils; large red quatrefoils; dots and V's and finally the red, white and grey kilim).

A parallel for the kilim is found in a shrine (A.III.13) where an identical pattern, but coloured black and white, covered earlier paintings of a hunting scene on the north wall. Finally no geometric or figurative paintings have so far been found in building-level II, from which only red panels survive.

Plates 33, 34

IX The enthroned goddess from the shrine in Level II, the latest found at Çatal Hüyük. Supported by two felines, the goddess is Mistress of Animals and is shown giving birth to a probably male child. She is made of baked clay and was found in the grain bin of the shrine

X Group of three statuettes in blue (left) and brown limestone, from shrine VI.A.10, showing the double aspect of the goddess, maiden and mother, accompanied by the divine child—all three statues in association with a leopard, the sacred animal of the deities of the animal world and of nature

XI Detail of a doe and fawn from the hunting scene in the ante-chamber of shrine A.III.1., the latest shrine with pictorial representations found at Çatal Hüyük

XII Burial of a woman with funeral gifts in shrine VI.B.20. On the left a round basket imprint in white, then a polished obsidian mirror set in lime plaster and just beyond it a small oval basket containing rouge

XIII Fragment from the southern part of the dancers painting on the east wall of shrine A.III.1, showing a hunter in white loin-cloth and black-spotted, pink leopard skin. Round the neck he wears a pendant and in his right hand he holds a bow

XIV Ceremonial dagger of flint from male burial in shrine VI.B.29. The dagger which is polished on one side and pressure-flaked on the other was provided with a carved bone handle representing a snake

XV Bead necklaces and bracelets of various cut and polished stones, mainly from Levels VI.A and B. Blue apatite necklace of beads in the form of stylized goddesses from a shrine IV.8 red ochre burial. Eye for fastening belt hooks, of polished bone, from a burnt burial in shrine VI.A.5

IX

X

XI

XII

XIII

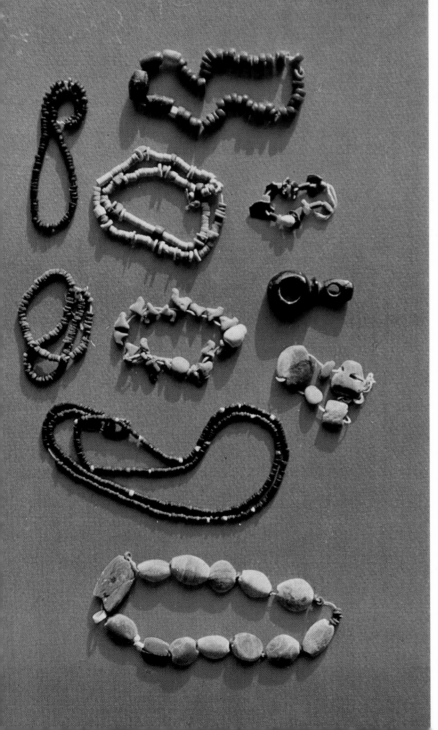

XIV

XV

Symbols are frequent in the wall-paintings of Çatal Hüyük and we have already had occasion to refer to them in the description of a number of paintings in Levels VI and III. Most motifs may have had a symbolic meaning and, among these, human hands and quatrefoils, probably a stylized flower, are at once the most prominent and the most ancient. The earliest fragment of a wall-painting from Çatal Hüyük, that found in the debris below a house of Level X, shows such a quatrefoil, shaped rather like a Maltese cross; this probably decorated the jamb of a doorway as do many others in Levels VII and VI B. They appear as fill-motifs in kilim paintings of Levels VI B and VI A, or decorate whole fields in rows in shrine A.III.8 described above.

Plate 36

Far more elaborate is a panel from shrine VI.A.66 where such flower-like motifs occur on either side of two others; an object resembling at first sight a 'double axe' and a mauve and orange wheeled cross with strange projections at the end of each arm. One of the arms overlies the flower on the right and the flower itself covers a crenellation pattern like those from the west wall of shrine A.III.8. Three small goddesses and two superimposed human figures, a steatopygous female and a male archer are painted between the wheeled cross and the flower pattern to the right. Although overpainting is notable, no layers of white paint intervened between these layers of paint and additions were therefore made to already existing paintings in the way of Upper Palaeolithic and many primitive paintings. At Çatal Hüyük this procedure is unique. It is impossible to extract the meaning from this painting as a whole, but we can at least make some suggestions about the symbols. As double axes are not found at Çatal Hüyük, there are no grounds for interpreting this symbol as a double axe. This strange shape finds its best parallels in a number of stone beads from the same building-level, and its association with stylized flowers might possibly suggest that some sort of insect (bee or butterfly) is meant. The small double triangles seen between the four petals of the flowers and beyond do not suggest that these are necessarily part of the flower, they look more like moths attracted by the flowers. One of the most common moths round Çatal Hüyük is the hummingbird moth, which flies by day,

Plate 40

and the 'double axe' may represent some bright butterfly, of which there are plenty in spring in the Konya Plain when the plain is studded with flowers.

The wheeled cross also presents difficulties and is unique at Çatal Hüyük. Could it represent four tall standing figures with upraised arms and legs combined into a circle—the four representing the points of the compass or the four regions of the plain—doing homage like the two human figures one of which covers her face to the thrice repeated mother goddess hovering in the distance? Does this wall-painting symbolize an act of homage to the great goddess on a spring morning in the Konya Plain amids fields of flowers and humming insect life nearly eight thousand years ago, or is this too fanciful an interpretation? It would be rash to deny the existence of agrarian rites in Neolithic religion; they are well attested in Minoan-Mycenaean and later Greek cults which owe so much to Anatolia.

Plate 39

There are, moreover, other paintings at Çatal Hüyük in shrine VI.B.8 (east wall) that again seem to depict fields of flowers and insect life. Two superimposed paintings depict versions of a single composition. The earlier, which is also the more complete, shows a cellular structure in red. On the left these cells are not filled with any design; in the central portion of the painting white circles, sometimes with a central dot, fill the cells and most of these on the right are filled with a flower-like pattern, parallel wavy lines, winged or wingless insects. The red cellular structure is part of the painting and not superimposed on it. The interpretation suggested was that of the life-cyle of the bee in a honeycomb with closed cells on the left, from which, in the middle, the bees emerge to fly freely in a field of flowers on the right. Rows of four-fingered human hands in pink and black along the top and in pink (vertical) and white (horizontal) along the bottom provide a frame for this intriguing picture.

Plate 42

The later wall-painting, superimposed on the other after a lapse of time was similar in composition, but only the southern end has survived. There are some differences however, the main one being that the cellular pattern is an addition to the original painting which shows a field of flowers and branches from which sway wingless

Plate 41

Fig. 46

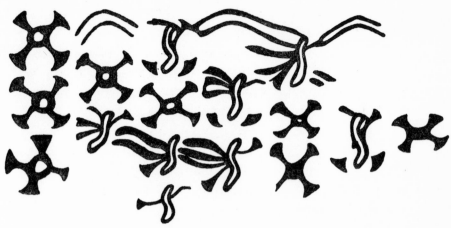

46 Copy of a later painting on the east wall of shrine VI.B.8 with the red net pattern removed showing insects and flowers. See Plates 41, 42

insects or chrysalises, whilst other insects or butterflies hover with clearly marked wings around the flowers. That this scene was inspired by nature is clear in spite of stylization and the subject is evidently spring (there are no flowers in the Konya Plain after the end of June). The most incongruous element in these paintings is the four-fingered hands and why are these four-fingered only here? One cannot help wondering why Neolithic man's most important crops—the spiked ears of wheat and barley—alone never appear in any of these wall-paintings. Could there be a remote symbolism connecting these hands with the ears of corn? Did neolithic man perhaps have the notion that the ears were the plant's hand where we talk about 'heads' or 'ears'. Why do we find this interest in plant and animal life in ritual wall-paintings but to man's interest and advantage?

We may perhaps suggest a different explanation for these scenes; the cycle of the agrarian year with the blank field on the left representing the fallow field; the circles and dots, the holes in which the seeds were planted; the flowers and insects, the emergence of the crops, and the red cellular net pattern with hands on either side a symbolic representation of the gathering of the fruit, in other words the harvest. The idea of 'netting the harvest' could easily have been

Plates 43, 44

derived from the other occupation of Neolithic man, the hunt in which nets were certainly used.

The association of hands and net-like patterns recurs in shrine VII.8, which lies directly below the building with the scenes just described. In a wall-painting which occupies part of the west and north walls we find the same association of red and black hands above and red hands below a series of alternate red and black linear net-like patterns. Here there are no fields of flowers, but there is a big black bull further along the north wall. Whether a connection exists between the two actual paintings is impossible to affirm and the bull could conceivably be somewhat later in date.

Still another shrine (VI.B.10) shows a net-like painting, with some hands added in a certain phase around the head of a bull above a niche, perhaps another symbolic attempt at capture. If translated to a religious sphere (conquest of death?), a parallel for this is found in the same building where a checkerboard pattern (another representation of a net?) surrounds a similar niche surmounted by the lower jaw of a boar, another death-symbol. Parts of red lines suggestive of nets or a stockade appear behind a bull on the north wall of shrine A.III.1 and two panels of painting on the north wall of shrine VI.B.15 show a black and red net-pattern, textile-like in precision and more regular than that of shrine VII.8. This is partly covered by another and larger panel with about three score hands, fifty-seven of which have survived. Finally it may not be a coincidence that the bulls' heads and the ram's head above the net and hand patterns on the east wall of shrine VI.B.8 are also painted with pictures of nets and hands, as if these animals, like the bull and the boar in the neighbouring building, were to be captured. Where this idea of net and animal occurs in shrines, it is on the east or north wall, traditionally associated with death and above the platforms beneath which the dead rested (this specific location also applies to the boar's jaw and niche in shrine VI.B.10).

A further panel of human hands left in reserve on a red background was found below the later of the two paintings discussed above on the east wall of shrine VI.B.8 and may have been associated with it. All the hands are those of adults and they look like hands held on the wall round which paint was applied, whereas most others (except those in house VI.A.63) were painted on the wall in a positive technique. Most hands at Çatal Hüyük are right hands, but there are a number of left hands. All are, however, complete hands and there are no signs of mutilation, such as are claimed for a number of representations in Upper Palaeolithic cave sanctuaries, especially Gargas in the Pyrenees. The curious empty circle in the palm which occurs on a large number of the Çatal Hüyük paintings is easily explained and is the result of pressing a hand dipped in paint on to the wall. If care is taken to press all fingers to the wall the centre of the palm does not touch it thus leaving a circle free of paint. The fact that so many hands are painted (and not impressed) in this way shows that the practice of dipping hands in paint was widespread and used, *e.g.*, on animal heads, goddess-figures, etc.

The interpretation of paintings or impressions of hands—and to this we may add one foot imprint—then is varied. There is either the idea of touching a sacred figure in search of protection, obtaining its blessing and warding off evil (which is implied in protection) or association of hands with other scenes suggests something quite different; it would appear to be an abbreviation for people, just as bulls' and rams' heads apply the same principle of *pars pro toto* for bull and ram. 'All hands' still has the same meaning today in many languages, and some of these paintings may be captioned 'All hands to the harvest' or 'All hands to the net' a way of expression that has survived the eight thousand years that separate us from the Anatolian Neolithic. There is probably no need to remind any reader that the harvest, that symbol of Neolithic achievement and man's delivery from hunger, still to this very day demands every available hand. It is man's hands which differentiate him from the animal, and this most versatile of instruments has made him what he is. That *Homo sapiens* should have realized this and given recognition and expression to it in his art is no less than we can expect. From Neolithic times onwards the hand became the symbol of creation, of effort, both human and divine, and of man himself. It is the hand which sought blessings in prayer, the hand which caressed and the hand which warded off evil.

Plate 7

Plate 39

Fig. 45

Plate 11

Plate 46

Paintings of human figures, goddesses and animals are comparatively rare at Çatal Hüyük. The goddess is usually represented in plaster reliefs, which may or may not have been painted. Three small goddesses, each with raised arms and upturned legs were found on the painting from shrine VI.A.66 already described, but a much larger one, about 61 cms in height, was found on the southernmost panel of the east wall of shrine VI.A.50 painted in monochrome red, showing the same familiar position. So far this is the only figure of a large goddess painted on the wall and not modelled in relief.

Leopards, attributes of the goddess, were found only in shrine VI.44 and these also were modelled in relief and painted; bulls, the symbol of the male deity, occur more frequently in relief than in paint. On the north wall of shrine IX.8 a large black bull was painted, only part of which has survived. Below its front hoof is a rectangular structure painted in red, the significance of which is not clear. The bulls on the north walls of shrines VII.8 and VI.8, cut into the plaster and painted, have already been described and the only remaining bull, that from shrine A.III.8, will be discussed below. Two fragmentary birds come from a broken panel on the east wall of house VI.B.34 and they may have been part of a larger scene destroyed by a deep Hellenistic pit, the stagnant water of which caused the downfall of this panel in antiquity.

Wall-paintings of vultures attacking human bodies are found only in three shrines of Levels VII and VIII and illustrate the preliminaries of the burial habits of the Neolithic population of Çatal Hüyük, which consisted of secondary burial of skeletons cleaned by vultures. These paintings are therefore of the utmost importance as they shed light on a practice which may have been far more widely practised than is commonly realized.

In the earliest painting, which comes from the east wall of shrine VIII.8 two large black vultures are shown, painted over the remains of an earlier polychrome kilim painting. Between them is a minute human figure, shown swinging a sling in vigorous motion, presumably to ward off the two vultures from the small headless corpse which lies on its left side to his right. In his left hand he is holding an object which may have been a mace or club. Behind the vulture on

the left there are more black slings and the indistinct remains perhaps of a further red figure. The lower part of the painting has been
destroyed by damp.

The second vulture painting decorated the north wall of shrine *Figs 14, 15*
VII.21. One complete group of two vultures, face to face over the
headless body of a human figure, survives, but beyond the post on Plate 47
the wall the wings of a further vulture were found which indicates
that the scene was probably repeated, but with only one vulture as
the presence of the doorway leaves no room for a pair. In this shrine
the entire scene was painted in a fine reddish-brown paint on a dead-
white background. The collapse of the wall has obliterated the tops
of the vultures heads, but the crests are clearly shown. With their
enormous wings, these gruesome creatures dwarf the small headless
human figure between them and this differs from all others in being
shown with uplifted arms and widespread legs, as if it were lying on
its back. A further peculiarity of this painting is seen in the legs of the
vultures which, far from being naturalistically drawn as in shrine
VII.8, are clearly those of human beings. The question therefore
arises whether these vultures really portray beasts of prey or human
beings disguised in vulture garb performing what is evidently a
funerary rite. For this there is plenty of evidence in the shrine, which
contained four human skulls.

It is not difficult to imagine the awe and terror which the wall-
paintings of shrine VII.8 must have inspired in Neolithic man, *c.*
6200 BC, on entering. All around its north and east wall, a great
frieze showed not less than seven vultures with outspread wings *Fig. 47*
making a feast of six small headless human beings. Vultures do
not remove skulls so that it may be assumed that the absence
of heads is a pictorial convention to indicate corpses. The burials
found below this gruesome scene were all anatomically intact
and none had lost their skulls, so there is no immediate connection between the burial-rites and the wall-painting in this shrine.
The corpses in the painting are shown in positions in which we find Plates 45, 48, 49
the dead are buried, either contracted on their left side or fully extended. Five large vultures are shown on the north wall and continue into the east wall up to the first post, and on the two large

panels of that wall even larger vultures are portrayed with wing-spans of about 5 feet, *i.e.* nearly life-size. The bird represented is probably the Griffon vulture (*Gyps vulvus*) of Anatolia, very frequently seen in the Konya Plain and a most useful bird in countries where the law forbids the burying of dead animals. These scenes speak for themselves and are evidently connected with the burial rite of excarnation for which there is abundant evidence at Çatal Hüyük. The beaks of vultures leave no marks on the bones, they only tear off the flesh, and the brain inside the skull is not disturbed.

Plate 8
Fig. 44

Disarticulated skulls and other elements of bodies occur in two wall-paintings from shrine VI.B.1. In the first of these, painted on the east wall, a jumble of human bones is shown reminiscent of a disturbed grave, and in the second a series of what looks like human skulls, or rather decomposing heads and some bones are shown below a construction of reeds and matting (described above, p. 65), which probably represents the mortuary where the rites of excarnation were practised, presumably well away from the site and probably upstream.

Plates 50, 51

In only one other building, a shrine (E.IV.1) of Level IV, is a scene presented which seems to be part of a funerary rite. Below the torso of a man (painted red) in a white loin-cloth (?) the head of a bearded man is shown and a little higher up towards the left there are the remains of what may have been a second head which, judging by the remains of a diadem of round discs, may have been that of a woman. This wall-painting is very badly destroyed, but there is certainly no room for two complete human figures and it seems far more likely that the red man was carrying two or more human heads. The carried head of the man is bearded and has a big lock of black hair; his grinning mouth and forehead are painted red as if smeared with blood and the eyes are closed. Other dabs of red are found on his cheeks, but no nose is indicated, and the impression one gets is that of a dead man.

Plate 53

Of the rest of the scene little can be made out except a small white figure with short legs, a plump torso and raised arms, another small white figure and two groups of white, red and black lines which defy interpretation in their present state. Of the paintings along the south

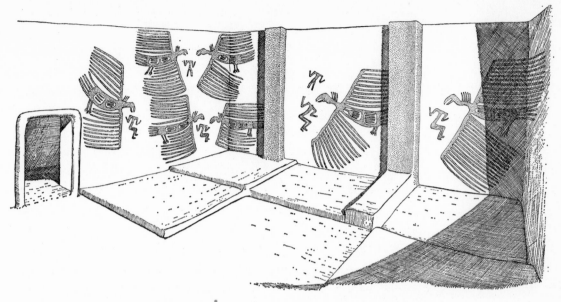

47 Earliest paintings on the north and east walls of the Vulture Shrine, VII.8. See Plates 45–48

wall only the legs of some figures painted in red are preserved, but they show that figures at least 18 cms in height were once painted on that wall. The state of preservation of the figures on the main panels of the east wall is most unsatisfactory, and only the upper part of a small red male figure now survives among a number of fragments of white persons or objects. To the right of the northern posts, decorated in one phase with black geometric patterns and later covered with red and white paint, a small standing figure of a woman in a leopard-skin dress, red necklace and red anklets is all that survived. Over the north-east platform remains of a hunting (?) scene fallen from the north wall on to the floor of the shrine could at least be drawn in reconstruction. Four male figures, wearing white garments and animal skins, are shown moving towards an unintelligible scene on the left, which looks like an animal (bear ?) trapped in a net. Beyond it another male figure extends a hand towards an animal head (?) and beyond that is a solid mass of red paint. There is evidence that the west wall of this shrine had also been ornamented with paintings, of which only specks survived. The destruction of this building, which was directly below the surface of the mound is most regrettable, for it is one of the very few decorated with a series of scenes in which human beings played a prominent part.

The only other wall-painting from a building of Level IV (A.IV.1) was found on the central post of its north wall. It is only a fragment but shows two running male figures and the now-headless figure of a bull, in front of the bull are the remains of a third human figure which is running or has fallen and is the object of the bull's attack. The other traces of indistinct figures belong to an almost obliterated later painting, the subject of which is no longer clear. The tall slender bodies, the long heads, the line of the hair shown in black are all similar to the human figures in shrine E.IV.1 and would seem to be characteristic of a style of paintings in building-levels IV and III.

Remains of a small but lively hunting scene were found on the walls of room A.III.13. Here a stag, accompanied by two fawns (one is lost but for its hind-legs), is pursued by a hunter and his dog. The man is shown at the point of releasing an arrow from his bow and the schematized rendering of the body has nevertheless captured this moment of haste and tension. His legs are bent and his animal-skin is floating behind him in the rush of action. The representation of a dog is the only proof for domestication of this animal at Çatal Hüyük. This painting was later coated with white plaster and part of it covered with a black and white kilim pattern.

Next to the small room with the hunting-scene lay the remains of a large shrine (A.III.1), which has yielded some of the finest wall-paintings yet found at Çatal Hüyük. These are also the latest, dating from about 5800 or a little after; let us say the first quarter of the fifty-eighth century BC. Like many of the buildings found directly below the surface of the mound this shrine had suffered much from Hellenistic intrusions which had damaged the greater part of the east and west wall. Its antechamber, decorated with a large deer-hunt, was remodelled after a fire and the wall-painting was cut back by an unknown amount. Only the greater part of the north wall with its painting of a bull was more or less intact, but this painting had suffered from roots and animal holes and had faded more than any other in the building.

Plate 52

Plates 56, 57

Fig. 48

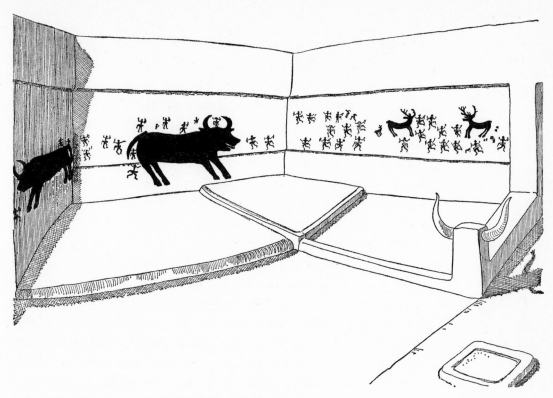

48 *Restoration of the main room of shrine A.III.1. See Plates 61–64*

Plates 54, 55, XI

The south wall of the antechamber bore the scene of a deer-hunt painted in monochrome red without any additions in other colours. It measured *c.* 1·5 metres in its present truncated state and was repainted four times with exactly the same pattern. The painting, now in the Ankara Archaeological Museum, is the second of the four (the first was badly destroyed and most fragmentary) and as this was the first wall-painting to be found at Çatal Hüyük, we are much indebted to Mr Ernest Hawkins, the Byzantologist, for his help and teaching us how to remove a wall-painting from a burnt mud-brick wall.

The scene shows five or six men, of different sizes, some naked and others dressed in animal-skins which project stiffly from the waist, armed with bows, slings or maces and a lasso (?), attacking a herd of Red Deer (*Cervus elaphus*). The herd consists of three stags, two does and two young fawns fleeing to the right of the picture. Many of the animals turn their heads towards their pursuers and in the bottom register a fine stag has been brought down by two of the men who are apparently preparing to kill it, while the leader of the hunt, drawn to a larger scale, fixes his attention on another large stag, above which a fragmentary small man appears. Two others are shooting arrows at the does. The scene is extremely lively even if the naturalism of the animals is tempered by pictorial stylization. Built into the new south wall of the room was a fragment, probably derived from the same scene, showing the feet of another large deer. It is unfortunately unknown how much of this painting has been lost, for it is conceivable that it covered not only the south but also the west wall of the antechamber before the alterations.

The south wall of the main room of the shrine had no wall-paintings, but a single stag was painted on the southernmost portion of the east wall on the middle panel some 61 cms above the floor. The lower panel was deeply recessed, and on its north wall remains were found of a painting in black, red and white, which, with

Plate 58

some ingenuity, could be restored into a fine stag's head, but this restoration is by no means certain.

The north wall of the building was decorated with a wall painting

Fig. 48

of which a great bull, 2·05 metres in length, occupied the centre. Its feet were painted on the lower panel and have not survived. Sur-

Plates 61, 62, 64

rounding the bull a number of running male figures were drawn, armed with bows and dressed in animal-skins. These were not only fragmentary, but in many cases their colours had faded and there were traces of over-painting. Two of these figures, one between the curving horns of the bull, the other far behind him, are painted half

Plate 62

red, half white. The first figure wears a red animal skin and is armed with a bow, the second wears a pink leopard skin with black spots and is waving a club or mace, and both are headless. The other hunters painted red originally had heads, though some have lost them as the paintings deteriorated.

Towards the west end of the north wall a group of hunters, including the headless figure in the leopard skin, are turned towards another animal, smaller than the large bull, that was painted on the west wall. Fragments of two hunters appear near his hind quarters and between them and two others are a number of red lines which may represent a net or stockade. This originally extended much further down, but as its fragments were found in a Hellenistic pit which had cut away the north-west corner (and most of the brick-work of the west wall) restoration, even on paper, remains somewhat uncertain. It seems extremely likely that a second and smaller bull surrounded by hunters once occupied the west wall up to the door-way. The entire scene of what is almost certainly a bull hunt (and not a scene of bull-worship) still measures 5·5 metres in its truncated state and was probably another metre or so in length originally. This painting was the earliest one on the north and west wall and thus dates from the earliest occupation of the shrine. Traces of repainting were found among the figures surrounding the big bull and patches of solid red paint covered the net and the hindquarters of the second animal. What they represented can no longer be ascertained.

The east wall of this shrine was originally decorated with a great panel 3·4 metres in length and 66 cms in height, set some 61 cms above the level of the two main platforms, and extending from the north-east corner to the wooden post. It showed scenes of dancing in connection with a deer hunt and not less than twenty-four human figures are wholly or partly preserved out of an unknown number. Of this exciting wall-painting only a large fragment (about 91 cms in length) was still *in situ* at the north end of the wall together with two other fragments, one along the top edge of the panel with the antler of one deer and the head of a second and four human figures, the second along its southern edge (1·2 metres in length) below the second stag. This piece had slipped into a Hellenistic trench together with numerous other fragments when the trench became water-logged. The arrangement of the small fragments in connection with the larger pieces, though based on the position in which they were found is therefore reconstruction rather than fact, but the result is entirely convincing. What we do not know is whether more figures were originally present in the open spaces left in the reconstruction, since, if there were originally more, their fragments have perished.

On the major fragment of the wall-painting three successive layers of painting were clearly recognizable: first, the earliest and best preserved, then a middle one with larger figures running towards the

Plate 61

Plate 63

right and a third and latest painting with two rather lifeless figures depicted in reddish-brown. In style these latest figures resemble some of those painted around the great bull, but they do not appear to be contemporary, as the bull-hunt is undoubtedly of the same period as the earliest deer-hunt. The latest of the three paintings on this wall being in monochrome and in a different style, was easy to recognize. A man in an animal-skin is shown holding two bows and behind him is a second man with a small animal (dog ?) before him. Nowhere else on this wall were further fragments of this painting found.

The middle painting is in polychrome and shows extremely lively figures larger than those of the lowest layer, running at great speed towards the right. They are dressed in pink leopard-skins with black spots and wear bonnets of the same material. Most of them are armed with bows or club. The object of their attention are probably the deer, which seem to have been repainted once. A number of figures of this phase are preserved in patches only over earlier ones, alas not enough to complete this scene, but it may be assumed that groups of hunters running towards the deer from both sides formed its subject.

Plate 61

The earliest painting is also the best preserved. The major fragment shows a scene that should probably be interpreted as a dance of the hunters. With the exception of two figures in the bottom register, a drummer and a bowman with raised sling, all the figures are shown proceeding to the left in three superimposed rows. The three figures in the middle row (there may have been more originally) are larger in size and the first is painted half red, half white, and is headless like the third figure which is all white except for a leopard-skin on the shoulder. The middle figure wears a white loin-cloth as well as a leopard-skin (pink with black spots) in which all figures except two naked acrobats are dressed. Similarly all figures wear berets of leopard-skin. They are armed with bows and slings and one figure in the top row is shown holding a small animal, possibly a dog. It appears that the dance takes place around the central figure in the middle and its purpose is possibly to insure the success of the hunt which is shown in the same panel further to the right. Here two stags and a fawn are shown, as well as a number of hunters all dressed in the same garb, and except one at the very end of the picture, all moving towards the left. No headless figures are found here, but one man placed below the stag in the middle of the scene is differently dressed in a pale yellow skin with white borders (lion- or deer-skin ?). Towards the far end of the painting a number of inexplicable objects appear; a skin (?) in front of the man below the second deer, deer's tracks (?) behind him and beyond that a poly-chrome design and two grinning human (?) heads above. Their meaning is obscure, but they tend to remind us that the wall-paint-ings at Çatal Hüyük were not art for art's sake, but had a ritual meaning.

Plate XIII

Two important questions remain to be answered: the relationship between the bull and the deer-hunt and the identity of the headless figures found in both paintings. Although it seems unlikely that bull and deer-hunt were painted by the same person it is probable that they are of the same date and it is by no means impossible that the two scenes are meant to be seen as one painting symbolizing the hunt. They more or less flow into each other and it will not have escaped notice that in the dancing scene the majority of the partici-pants advance towards the left, *i.e.* towards the bull, who for sheer size and magnificence dominates the entire composition. In a way the deer on the right are balanced by the second animal on the far left, and in both hunts we find the mysterious headless harlequins. When we compare these with the headless corpses of the vulture paintings, the interpretation of these figures as dead ancestors may gain some credence. That great hunters of the past were invoked to partake in the hunting-rites of the living does not strain one's credulity and the only way of indicating their status was to show them headless and parti-coloured. As it seems extremely unlikely that the entire popula-tion, or even all the males, were dressed in leopard-skins, we may assume that the hunters here represented were a small section of the populace entitled to this ceremonial dress, in other words the priesthood. It seems unlikely that at this period the entire able manhood of Çatal Hüyük, which must run into the thousands, partook in annual hunting-rites and it is far more likely that the conduct of such rites was entrusted to a select body of priests. That

Fig. 48

this shrine was devoted to the hunt seems beyond reasonable doubt and it may be significant that the second shrine nearby was entirely decorated with floral symbols and kilims, symbols of agriculture and weaving, occupations pre-eminently associated with women. Nor is it probably a coincidence that the shrine of Level II was built on top of this latter building and that stamp-seals and grain as well as nine female statuettes should have been found in the building, which may have still been reserved for women. The hunting-shrine of Level III soon lost its early decoration and about thirty to thirty-five layers of white plaster covered its paintings, which belonged to the first years of its use. In Level II the shrine was not rebuilt and with the decline in hunting came the decay of the obsidian industry in Level II. Sometime during the fifty-eighth century BC agriculture finally triumphed over the age old occupation of hunting and with it the power of woman increased: this much is clear from the almost total disappearance of male statues in the cult, a process which, beginning in Çatal Hüyük II, reaches its climax in the somewhat later cultures of Hacılar.

Wall-painting also came to an end and the painting of pottery took its place, but with the greatly reduced space for painting animals, deities and figures were broken down and stylized almost beyond recognition in the 'fantastic style' of Hacılar; only hands and textile patterns survived unchanged for another five hundred years.

Plates 59, 60

There remains but a single wall-painting to be described, which more than any other illustrates the artistic genius of the people of Çatal Hüyük. Painted on the north and east wall of a shrine (VII.14) of Level VII, soon after 6200 BC according to radiocarbon dating, it represents that rarest genre of early painting, a landscape and needless to say it is unique. In the foreground is shown a town with rect-angular houses of varying sizes with internal structures reminiscent of Çatal Hüyük houses clearly indicated. Each house has its own walls and they are placed one next to the other without any open spaces. The rows of houses rise in terraces up to the top of the mound (as in the section of Level VI B and no doubt VII also).

Beyond the town and much smaller as if far away, rises a double peaked mountain covered with dots and from its base parallel lines extend. More lines erupt from its higher peak and more dots are grouped beyond its right slope and in horizontal rows above its peak, interspersed with horizontal and vertical lines. A clearer picture of a volcano in eruption could hardly have been painted: the fire coming out of the top, lava streams from vents at its base, clouds of smoke and glowing ash hanging over its peak and raining down on and beyond the slopes of the volcano are all combined in this painting. It is not difficult to localize this picture: Hasan Dağ (10,673 feet) is the only twin peaked volcano in Central Anatolia and it lies at the eastern end of the Konya Plain, within view of Çatal Hüyük. The Central Anatolian volcanoes became extinct only in the second millennium BC. Moreover, these volcanoes and Hasan Dağ especially, were the source of much raw material, in particular that of obsidian, for Çatal Hüyük, a source from which the site probably derived much of its wealth. It may be surmised that it was not only for its great cutting power, its transparency, reflective power and its jet black appearance that this material was so highly prized. Its volcanic and thus chthonic origin would have linked it to the underworld, the place of the dead, and it was a true gift of mother earth, and therefore imbued with magical potency. These considerations may help in explaining why an artist late in the seventh millennium BC recorded the wonder and awe of a volcanic eruption against the foreground of the town of Çatal Hüyük on the wall of one of its shrines. If the picture is unique so was the occasion and probably only at Çatal Hüyük had Neolithic people reached the necessary degree of civilization or possessed the artistic genius to record such an event for posterity.

Plate I

VIII

Sculpture in the Round

Besides the wall-paintings and plaster reliefs that decorate the majority of shrines and a number of houses, the people of Çatal Hüyük practised sculpture in the round in the form of stone and clay statuettes depicting their deities in anthropomorphic or near-anthropomorphic form. None of these is more than 30 cms in height and most are considerably smaller, varying from 5 to 20 cms on the average. The materials out of which such small cult statues were fashioned vary from terracotta to soft calcite, chalk, pumice and alabaster and from limestone to volcanic rocks and white marble. Bone tools were used for modelling, obsidian and flint tools cut the rock. For polishing, sand, crushed volcanic glass (obsidian) and perhaps emery were available, but all these raw materials with the exception of clay had to be brought from beyond the limits of the Konya Plain. The techniques were probably the same as those for the preparation of polished axes and adzes, maceheads, stone vessels, pendants and beads, and much labour could be saved by carefully choosing suitable boulders out of which the statues were to be cut.

Like many artists from the Upper Palaeolithic to the present, those of Çatal Hüyük appreciated the weird and suggestive shapes of natural rock formations, stalactites, stalagmites, limestone concretions or strangely weathered stones. It does not require an overdose of imagination to imagine a host of deities, humans or petrified animals in the grandeur of one of the stalagmitic caves, of which plenty were available in the Taurus Mountains. That Neolithic people visited such caves is clear from the fact that broken-off stalactites were deposited in the shrines together with cult statues on every occasion. Many indeed resemble clusters of breasts, udders or even human figures and it was obviously because of this resemblance, however remote to us, that they were collected and carried back to the shrines.

On more than one occasion, a resemblance was enhanced by some elementary sculpting. A block of limestone resembling a male riding an animal had a head carved on it; in another case a fearful image was created by carving a fine head on a knobbly limestone concretion. Limestone pebbles and boulders have incised features which turn them into shapes strangely resembling modern sculpture.

Plate 65
Plate 69

Plate 72

Often a little carving suffices to turn a pebble into a schematic seated goddess, but far more often naturalistic figures are carved out of a block of stone that can have had no previous resemblance to the final product. It would be utterly wrong to assume a line of typological development from aniconic, semi-aniconic to naturalistic image at least for this Early Neolithic period at Çatal Hüyük. All three forms occur side by side in the same buildings and a typological approach can only lead to chaos and misunderstanding. What strikes one most in the stone sculpture of this site is its diversity and the lack of what might be called a dominant style. A further factor to be borne in mind is the sacredness of a cult image. Unlike the wall-paintings which were covered with plaster or the reliefs which were desecrated when a shrine was filled in, cult-statues were not left in a shrine when it was abandoned. They were removed and taken to another shrine and carefully preserved like the cult-statues in our churches. As the result, it is quite as possible theoretically to find cult-statues, made let us say in Level VIII, in a shrine of Level VI as it is to find a Romanesque sculpture of the Crucifixion or a Flemish primitive in a Baroque church. The building in which it is found does not necessarily date the object. As many of the Çatal Hüyük statues are made of very durable stone, it is theoretically possible that many are much older than the buildings in which they were preserved as heirlooms, still magically potent, of a more remote past. It is therefore possible to argue that many of the stalactites, semi-aniconic figures, schematic figures, etc., need not be contemporary with the fine naturalistic statues with which they are found, but may be the remains of much earlier periods. On the other hand, such a procedure is arbitrary and is based on the preconceived idea of a typological development for which we have as yet no evidence whatsoever. The only proper solution to this problem is the location of the workshops in which the statues were made and only then will it be possible to establish a firm chronological sequence. In the meantime we must accept the possibility that stylistically utterly different types of statues were produced side by side. In Late Neolithic Hacılar VI we again find highly naturalistic clay statues side by side with menhir-like slabs of stone. Both show the same treatment of hair, eyes and nose and they are evidently contemporary with each other, in spite of the primitive crudity of the work in stone. Different functions, unfamiliarity with a new material and a quantity of other unknown factors may account for such stylistic discrepancies. Such factors are more likely to mislead the art-historian than the archaeologist, who is less concerned with grouping and stylistic classification than with the general cultural context.

From the context in which these statues are found it is clear that they served as cult-statues in the shrines and embodied the various deities, or aspects of deities, worshipped by the Neolithic population. With very few exceptions, these statues only occur in shrines in contrast to crude clay figurines, mainly of animals but including clumsy and highly schematized human figures, that are never found inside shrines but are stuck between the bricks or walls of shrines or occur in groups in pits near them. The contrast between statuettes and crude figurines is not only artistic but functional, and whereas the first probably represent cult-statues the second are ex-voto figurines left by worshippers or, as in the case of wounded and intentionally broken animal figurines, substitute representations of game magically killed or disabled in a hunting ritual.

Plate 66

The cult statuettes found in the shrines are a most valuable source for the reconstruction of Neolithic religion at Çatal Hüyük, and in contrast to most other Neolithic sites they do not entirely consist of 'Mother Goddesses', but also show a male deity. Moreover, many of these statuettes occur in groups, carved in the same material and sometimes with stylistic affinities, possibly made by the same sculptor. They are anything but uniform and one definitely has the impression that different aspects of the deities are stressed. Various ages, *hieros gamos* (ritual marriage), pregnancy, birth, command over wild animals, etc., are all clearly defined and many of the statuettes tell a story besides simply representing the goddess or the god; they refer to a certain episode in the life of the deities or they more clearly define a well-known association. This explicitness is a characteristic of both Çatal Hüyük and Hacılar and may have been typical of Neolithic Anatolian religion in general.

To avoid a tedious and lengthy description of the fifty or so statuettes discovered at Çatal Hüyük so far, they have been listed together with information on the material of which they are made, their height and findspot on pp. 202–3. From the same list it is evident that statues of a female deity far outnumber those of the male deity, who moreover, does not appear to be represented at all after Level VI. Most of the statuettes from the early levels (VII, VI) were carved in stone, whereas in the later levels (IV–II) the majority are modelled in clay and baked. The features are generally more naturalistically rendered and this naturalism is evidently the result of a long tradition of modelling in clay. Coarser clay figurines already appear in Level IX, remaining virtually unchanged throughout the period.

Characteristic of Çatal Hüyük is the representation of deities in human form where cult statuettes are concerned, whereas in the plaster sculpture and wall-painting only the goddess is thus portrayed. There can be little doubt that the Neolithic people of Çatal Hüyük conceived their deities in human form endowed with supernatural power over their attributes and symbols taken from a familiar animal world. As a symbol of male fertility an aurochs bull or a large ram was more impressive than man himself and the power of wild life and death was suitably symbolized in the leopard, the largest and fiercest wild animal in the region; in the destructive ferocity of the boar or in the impressive spectacle of flocks of Griffon vultures. Nothing suggests that these animals themselves were regarded as gods. Just as Neolithic man had learned (or was learning) to dominate nature through animal domestication and agriculture, so the power of his deities over wild life was clearly expressed in his sculpture. Leopards support the goddess in her confinement; leopard-cubs rest on her shoulders and leopard-skins clothe her. Two goddesses of different age stand behind leopards, patting their backs, and the boy-god is shown riding another, a convincing picture of the Divine

Plates 67, 68, IX;
Fig. 49
Plate 87; *Fig. 50*

Plates 73–76, X
Plate 86

181

49 *Clay statuette of a goddess holding two leopard cubs. From shrine A.III.1*

Fig. 26

Plates 18–20, VI

Fig. 23

Family; mother, daughter and son as Mistresses and Master of wild animals. A similar scene decorated the west wall of shrine VII.8 and a pair of leopards, male and female, modelled in relief and painted was found in shrine VI.B and A.44. In another case, shrine VII.1, a bull and a cow take the place of leopards and the emphasis here may be on a domesticated or domesticable species.

The frequency with which the goddess is shown associated with wild animals probably reflects her ancient role as the provider of game for a hunting population, and as patroness of the hunt. Her statuettes alone were found in the hunting shrine of Level III. Animal figurines, wounded or maimed in effigy during a hunting ritual, were found in pits near shrines VI.B.12 and IV.4, both of which contained plaster reliefs or statuettes of goddesses. Her association with possibly domesticated animals has been noted and her power over plant life and hence agriculture is clear not only

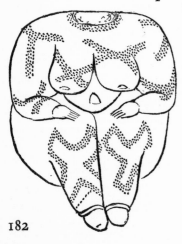

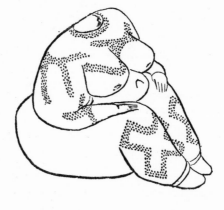

50 *Painted clay figure o, a goddess. From shrine VI.A.61. See Plate 79*

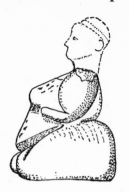

51 Painted clay statuette of a goddess in a leopard skin dress. From shrine E.IV.4

from the numerous representations of floral and vegetable patterns, painted on her figure or in her shrines, but also from the association of her statuettes in heaps of grain and crucifers in shrine VI.A.44 (the Leopard Shrine) and the discovery of the birth-giving goddess in a grain-bin of the Level II shrine. Here again the presence of the statue suggests a rite of sympathetic magic. The decoration of the second shrine of Level III, ornamented entirely with floral patterns or textile designs, suggests that she was regarded as much as an agrarian deity as a patroness of weaving, innovations of supreme importance for the Neolithic period. Her association with life has its inevitable counterpart in her association with death. She is shown giving birth to a son, represented in human form or as a bull or ram in the numerous shrines, and the immediately preceding stage, pregnancy, is as much in evidence in the statuettes as in the plaster reliefs. As a probable goddess of death, she is accompanied by a bird of prey, possibly a vulture and her grim expression suggests old age, the crone of later mythology. Her symbols of death, vultures, are frequently represented in early shrines (see pp. 166f.), and an elaborate symbolism, foreshadowing the words 'in the midst of life there is death', finds plastic expression in mother's breasts which incorporate skulls of vultures, fox and weasel or the lower jaws of boars with enormous tusks, eminently symbolic of the scavengers which thrive on death. A firm belief in afterlife is well attested by the burial customs and amulets of the goddess (highly stylized and graded in diminishing sizes like the similar Magdalenian figures from Petersfels

Plate 79; *Fig. 50*

Plates 67, 68

Plates 31–34

Plates 67, 68, IX; *Fig. 52*

Plate 77; *Fig. 53*

Plates 80, 82

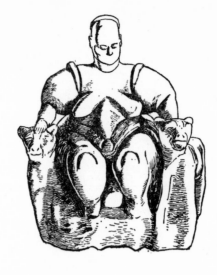

*52 Clay statuette of a goddess
supported by leopards giving
birth. From a grain-bin in shrine
A.II.1. See Plates 67, 68, IX*

Plate 81

in Baden) which covered the neck of a red-ochre burial in Level IV.
Other amulets show bulls' heads representing the male deity. So even
in death the protection of the deities was sought and the care of the
dead suggests the idea of resurrection, the denial of death, the tenet of
Plate 65 all religion. The stalactite goddess probably also stresses the idea
of chthonic power and the underworld.

If the goddess presided over all the various activities of the life and
death of the Neolithic population of Çatal Hüyük, so in a way did her
son. Even if his role is strictly subordinate to hers, the male's role in
Plate 83 life appears to have been fully realized. A small stone plaque shows a
couple in embrace on the left and mother with child, the offspring
of the union on the right. The birth of a god is frequently portrayed

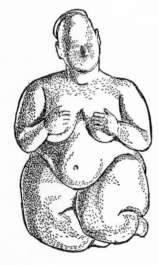

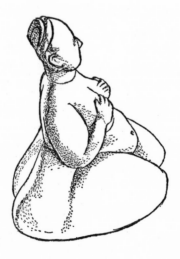

*53 Complete clay statuette of a
seated goddess. From shrine
A.II.1*

84, 85 Male deities, though not as prominent as their female counterpart, are still a feature of neolithic Çatal Hüyük. The proud adolescent figure, *above*, found with the Death Goddess and her vulture in shrine VI.A.25, seems characteristic of the confidence, pride and virility of the male at Çatal Hüyük, still a figure to be reckoned with and not yet entirely subservient to the wiles of women, as at Hacılar. The second white marble figure, *below*, shows a seated male wearing a cap of leopard skin and multiple bracelets worn above the elbow. Presumably he represents an aspect of hunting, which alone was responsible for the presence of an independent male deity in the neolithic of Çatal Hüyük

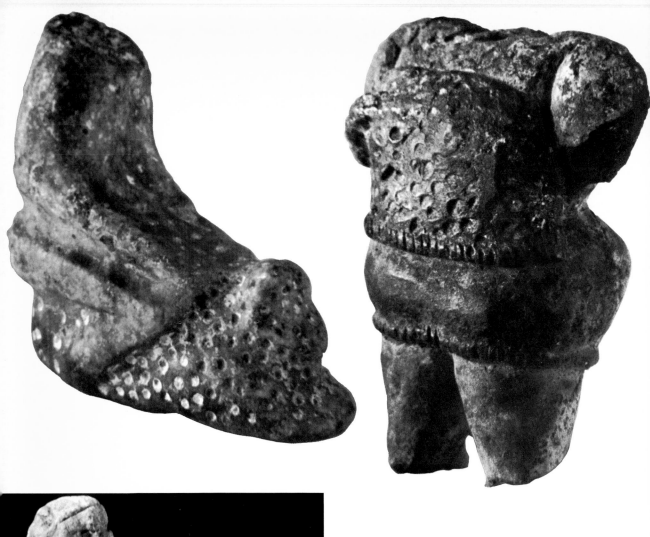

86–91 Of the six statuettes illustrated here only one is definitely female, *above right*. Made of baked clay it represents a young woman dressed in a blouse of leopard skin and a fringed woollen skirt and was found in shrine A.II.1. Four of the five male gods shown are seated on animals: the boy god, *above left*, part of the group in Plates 73–76 has already been described; a bearded male seated on a bull, *left*, from the Leopard Shrine (VI.A.44), and the white

calcite figure on a bull from shrine VII.21, the rear view of which is shown, *above*. The blue limestone bearded god on a bull, *right*, was found in shrine VI.A.10 together with the figure, *above right*, of a person in a long garment. Two of male figures are bearded and therefore probably represent the Goddess's husband, whereas the younger figures probably represent her son, the boy god, or her adolescent lover

92, 93 The people of neolithic Çatal Hüyük buried their dead below the platforms of houses, *above*, and shrines, *opposite*, alike, ·but only after the flesh had decomposed or had been removed by vultures or other natural agents. The bones, still in anatomical context, were wrapped up in cloth, or matting, and then deposited in earth graves below the platforms of their ancient homes. When a building was inhabited for a length of time, several burials would take place one on top of the other (house VI.B.34, *above*) often leading to the disturbance of earlier skeletons. In other cases, shrine VI.8, *opposite*, individual skeletons with their funerary gifts are easily disentangled

94, 95 In one unusual burial in shrine VI.1, the brains had been removed from the skull and a wad of fine cloth substituted, *above*. As the building above was destroyed by fire the action of the heat was sufficient to ensure carbonization of the material. A burial from shrine VI.7, *below*, has as a bracelet, dentalium beads and a red-painted basket as grave goods

96, 97 *Above*, burials found below the main (female) platform of house E.IV.1 with the latest burial semi-intact on the left and a row of displaced earlier skulls beyond. *Below*, a woman's skull decorated with a broad band of cinnabar from shrine VI.B.20, one of the relatively few ochreburials

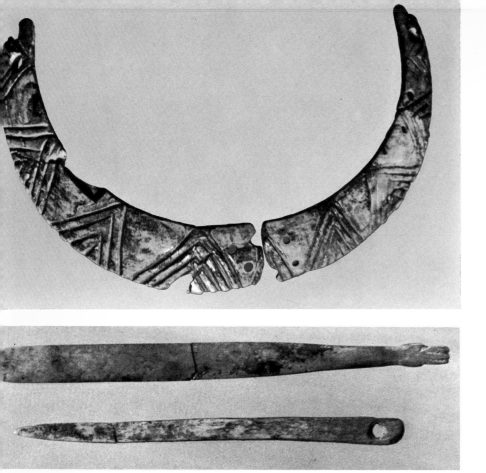

98–102 Male and female funeral gifts. *Above*, a fine collar of boar's tusk, incised and perforated, from a female burial in house VII.12. A bone spatula ending in a human hand and a bone bodkin came from a female burial in house IV.11. *Below*, finely polished bone belt-hooks and an eye for fastening a belt were found with male burials in shrines VI.A and B.20. *Above right*, a two pronged fork and, *below right*, two spatulae from houses A.III.2, B.II.1 and shrine E.IV.4, respectively

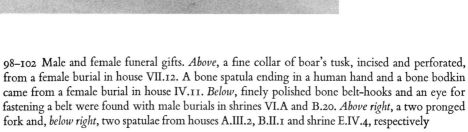

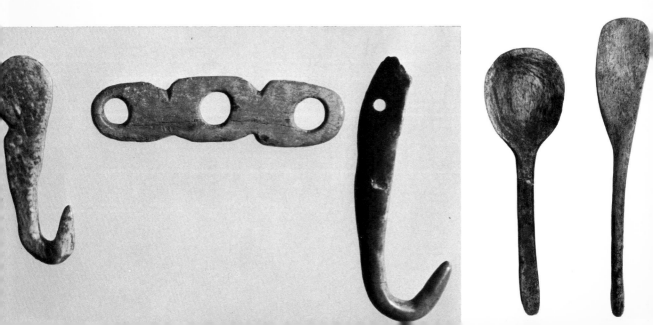

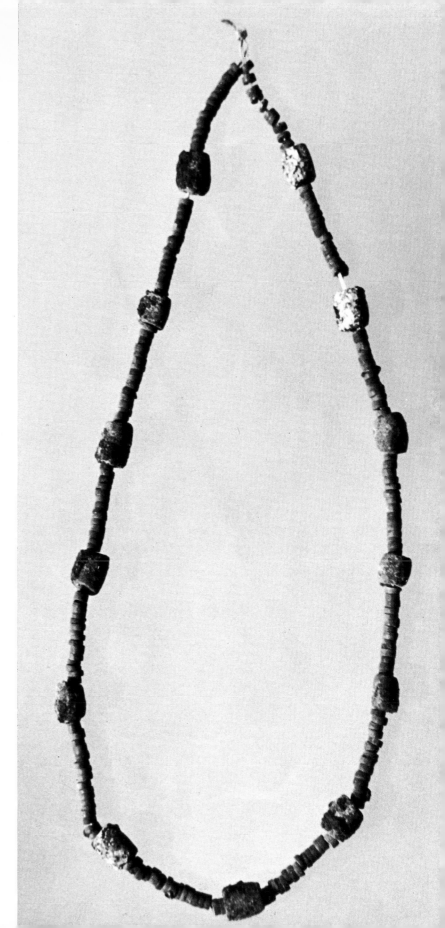

103, 104 Above, a bracelet of red and white small stone beads, blue and white limestone tubular beads and six deer teeth from the burial of a woman in house IX.1. *Right*, a necklace of black limestone beads and large beads of lead, from the burial of a young woman in shrine VI.A.10

105–108 In many instances wooden vessels were extremely well preserved at Çatal Hüyük VI, not only in graves, but some even in burnt buildings, *below*. The most outstanding products are boxes with closely fitting lids, *above*, rectangular (from shrine VI.A.1) or oval (from shrine VI.10). These were carved out of blocks of wood without any joinery or gluing. The lids are usually provided

with a small lug which serves as a handle (*below*). Handles were also carved on the large oval meat dish, *opposite below*, from shrine VI.61, nearly 50 cm. long. Oval bowls were very common, the oval box *above*, came from shrine VI.10, and they varied in shape and depth, some were like sauceboats, others boat-shaped

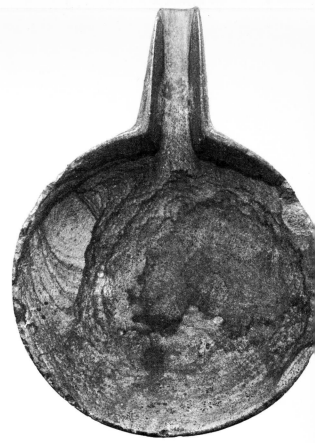

109–112 Three examples of pottery and a stone vessel from Çatal Hüyük: a straight-sided cream burnished bowl from Level II, *above left*; a dark burnished ware cooking pot with two ledge handles from house IV.8, *centre*, and a jar on four feet from house A.III.14, *below*, decorated with faint diagonal stripes of paint. Stone vessels were a luxury at Çatal Hüyük, a good example is the spouted dish of red sandstone, *above*, from shrine VI.A.8

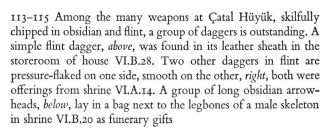

113–115 Among the many weapons at Çatal Hüyük, skilfully chipped in obsidian and flint, a group of daggers is outstanding. A simple flint dagger, *above*, was found in its leather sheath in the storeroom of house VI.B.28. Two other daggers in flint are pressure-flaked on one side, smooth on the other, *right*, both were offerings from shrine VI.A.14. A group of long obsidian arrowheads, *below*, lay in a bag next to the legbones of a male skeleton in shrine VI.B.20 as funerary gifts

116–118 Textile fragments from burials in shrine VI.A.5. *Above*, cloth tapes served to tie up the bundles wrapped in cloth; *centre*, woollen cloth with tabby weave covered a long bone of one of the skeletons in a shrine, but apart from this plain woven cloth there were other weaves such as the shawl or fish net weave of the piece shown *below*

119 Coiled baskets occur in all building-levels of neolithic Çatal Hüyük and they served every possible purpose; they were used for gathering food, for the storage of grain, contained jewellery and toilet articles or were used for burials of infants, children and even adults, *right*, from shrine VI.B.20

120 Rushes were in common use as a floor covering, but they were usually placed below woven mats, made from marsh grass which produced a very fine weave. Both are visible in the floor covering of shrine VI.A.14, *left*, with carbonized matting on the left and the white decayed reeds on the right

121 Baked clay seals are a prominent feature of the neolithic at Çatal Hüyük and they occur from Level VI B to Level II. They have a flat lower surface and bear incised patterns, among which spirals and especially meanders or meandroids are most common. Most are oval, round or sub-rectangular, but one exhibits a flower shape, so common from the textile paintings. They could have been used for stamping patterns on plain cloth rather than for painting the human skin, as is often assumed

in the shrines and once in a statuette. Differences in age distinguish between the god as son (the boy god on the leopard, the adolescent god); the hunter in a leopard skin cap or the consort-husband, who is shown bearded and seated on his symbol, the bull.

Plates 84, 86

Plate 85

Plates 88, 89, 91

This same distinction in age is made a number of times in representing the goddess as mother or daughter (the group with the leopards, the pair from the leopard shrine in black volcanic stone) or, occasionally as a twin figure which finds a parallel in the large twin plaster goddess on the west wall of shrine VI.14. Here the idea of pairs is twice shown; one of the two goddesses gives birth to a large and a small bull's head, son and consort. In other cases age is shown by absence of breasts, more mature contours, hood and cloak, etc., all of which would be immediately obvious to Neolithic people.

Plates 73–76, X

Plates 70, 71

Fig. 32

Plate 90

The divine family then was patterned on that of man; and the four aspects are in order of importance: mother, daughter, son and father. The question now arises whether Neolithic people worshipped these as four divinities or as two, for mother and daughter (or perhaps girl and mother) are but two aspects of the concept woman; son and father that of man. It would be extremely difficult to decide in this matter, but the general feeling one gets from the material favours the existence of but two deities: the Great Goddess and her son and paramour. Later parallels from Crete and Bronze Age Greece would tend to confirm this conception of the Divine family (Demeter, Kore or Persephone, and child Ploutos, as in the case of the exquisite ivory from the acropolis at Mycenae), the reference to the 'Two Ladies' in the Knossos texts and the dual role of Cretan Zeus, Phrygian Attis and Phoenician Adonis, associated with only one main goddess in the pattern of the dying and reviving god. It must be emphasized though, that the idea of a dying god does not appear to derive originally from Anatolia, and was probably unknown in the Anatolian Neolithic.

What is particularly noteworthy in the Neolithic religion of Anatolia, and this applies to Çatal Hüyük as much as to Hacılar, is the complete absence of sex in any of the figurines, statuettes, plaster reliefs or wall-paintings. The reproductive organs are never shown, representations of phallus and vulva are unknown, and this is the more remarkable as they were frequently portrayed both in the Upper Palaeolithic and in the Neolithic and Post-neolithic cultures outside Anatolia. It seems that there is a very simple answer to this seemingly puzzling question, for emphasis on sex in art is invariably connected with male impulse and desire. If Neolithic woman was the creator of Neolithic religion, its absence is easily explained and a different symbolism was created in which breast, navel and pregnancy stand for the female principle, horns and horned animal heads for the male. In an early Neolithic society like that of Çatal Hüyük one might biologically expect a greater proportion of women than men and this is indeed reflected in the burials. Moreover, in the new economy a great number of tasks were undertaken by the women, a pattern that has not changed in Anatolian villages to this day, and this probably accounts for her social pre-eminence. As the only source of life she became associated with the processes of agriculture, with the taming and nourishing of domesticated animals, with the ideas of increase, abundance and fertility. Hence a religion which aimed at exactly that same conservation of life in all its forms, its propagation and the mysteries of its rites connected with life and death, birth and resurrection, were evidently part of her sphere rather than that of man. It seems extremely likely that the cult of the goddess was administered mainly by women, even if the presence of male priests is by no means excluded, and such rare objects as obsidian mirrors, leopard-skins and finely wrought belt-fasteners may have been part of the ritual paraphernalia of female and male priests.

List of Sculptures

li. limestone; ma. marble (white); sc. schist; ba. basalt or volcanic stone; cl. clay; ca. calcite; al. alabaster. Heights are in centimetres.

Goddess

		Material	cms	shrine	plates
1. Semi-aniconic concretion with head.	Chthonic, cave or mountain aspect	li.	19·6	VIA.10	65
2. Pebble figures	Pregnant (?) goddess	li	16·0	VIA.10	
			11·7	VIA.10	69
3. Kneeling goddess with bird (vulture?)	Goddess of death	ma.	17·0	VIA.25	

Goddess		Material	cms	shrine	plates
4. Broken figure holding something	Mother and child (?)	ma.	9·5	VIA.10	
5. Twin Goddess	Mother and daughter	ma.	16·4	VIA.10	70, 71
6. Goddess and god in embrace	Ritual marriage	sc.	11·5	VIA.30	83
7. Goddess holding child	Mother and child	sc.	11·5	VIA.30	83
8. Pair of goddesses	Mother and daughter	ba.	16·3	VIA.44	
		ba.	12·0	VIA.44	
9. Pair of goddesses, male child and leopards	Mother, daughter and son as mistress and master of animals	li.	11·0	VIA.10	73–76
		li.	10·5	VIA.10	
		li.	5·5	VIA.10	86
10. Seated goddess with two leopard cubs	Mistress of animals	cl.	7·0	A.III.1	Fig. 49
11. Seated goddess giving birth		cl.	16·5	A.II.1	67, 68, IX
12. Seated goddess, dressed in leopard skin (painted)		cl.	6·0	IV.5	Fig. 50
13. Standing goddess, dressed in skirt and leopard blouse		cl.	5·0	A.II.1	87
14. Seated goddess, painted with flowers		cl.	4·1	VIA.61	79
15. Cloaked and hooded goddess		li.	8·0	VIA.10	90
16. Goddess with mouth and pendant breasts		li.	7·8	VIA.10	
17. Goddess in flounced robe (?)		ca.	5·3	VIA.25	
18. Goddess seated on something		ca.	4·2	VII.24	
19. Squat goddess		al.	5·1	VIB.45	
20. Crude chalk goddess		ch.	6·0	VIA.44	
21. Schematic seated goddess (no head)		li.	4·5	VIA.44	
22. Schematic goddess with arms on breast		ma.	5·0	VIA.10	72
23. Seated goddess with crossed legs		ma.	6·5	A.III.1	
24. Miniature seated goddess with crossed legs		ma.	3·0	A.III.1	
25. Standing pregnant goddess		al.	12·7	E.IV.5	77
26. Standing goddess		li.	5·5	A.II.1	
27–33. Group of seven seated goddesses		cl.	5–8·0	A.II.1	Fig. 53

God					
1. Child god riding leopard	Master of animals	li.	5·5	VIA.10	73–76, 86
2. Adolescent god seated on stool	Son of goddess	ma.	21·5	VIA.25	84
3. Seated god with leopard cap	Son and hunter	ma.	12·0	VIA.10	85
4. Seated god, bearded	Consort	al.	9·8	VIA.44	
5. God on bull	Consort (?)	ca.	c. 19·0	VII.21	89
6. Bearded god on bull	Consort (?)	al.	10·7	VIA.44	88
	Consort (?)	li.	11·0	VIA.10	91
7. Semi-aniconic god on animal	Consort (?)	li.	10·0	VII.24	
8. Twin (?) god on bull (?) fragment		ca.	6·0	VI.23	

IX

Burial-customs and Grave-goods

THE NEOLITHIC PEOPLE of Çatal Hüyük buried their dead below the platforms of houses and shrines and only rarely below any other part of the floor. No burials have been found in storerooms or courtyards and extramural burial, such as was found at aceramic Hacılar *c.* 7000 BC, was apparently unknown at Çatal Hüyük.

It is now clear that secondary burial was practised at this site, *i.e.* the skeletons were stripped of soft tissues before burial inside the dwellings, probably not just for simple reasons of hygiene but part of a highly developed pattern of rites of passage. Upon death the corpse of the deceased was probably removed to a mortuary outside the settlement where vultures cleaned the corpses down to the bones and dry ligaments. Presumably the dead were exposed on platforms, accessible to the birds and insects, but not to dogs and other scavengers which carry off bones. Evidently care was taken to preserve the skeleton intact in anatomical position and a check was kept on their identity. Whether this was the duty of the relatives or that of a special class of undertakers is of course not known, but the former seems more likely. To strip the flesh of the unborn child found in shrine VI.14 other methods were evidently used, such as immersion in a pot of water for only in this way could the minute bones survive intact. In a fair number of skeletons the brain was still in the skulls, but in one instance it was removed and a ball of fine cloth substituted.

It seems extremely likely that the burial of the dead coincided with the annual spring or early summer redecoration of houses and shrines, when the population must have found other quarters for the duration of the burial rites, the white-washing and the time required for the plaster to dry out thoroughly. This implies that the dead were kept in the mortuary until the annual ceremony and it is therefore not surprising to find some differences in the state of excarnation of the

Plate 8

Plate 94

corpses. Some had lost fingers or toe bones or the head had become detached whereas others still contained human fat and traces of flesh at the time when the burials took place. Some skeletons were more or less disjointed whereas others were still anatomically intact with not a single bone out of place. From the preservation of perishable materials, such as cloth, skin, fur, etc., frequently preserved below the skeletons it is clear that they were buried only when they had reached a state of complete or near desiccation. Wrapped in cloth or skins fastened with cloth straps and leather thongs or fibre rope, the skeletons were buried below the platforms at an average depth of 60 cms, sometimes laid on mats but more often directly in the earth. The edges of the platforms served as a demarcation line and no burial protruded beyond them, but where for lack of space the dead were buried below the floor they were put in oval graves.

Plate 119

No definite orientation was observed, but the head is usually turned towards the centre of the building and the feet towards the wall. Most, but not all the dead lie on their left side in a contracted position but some are extended on their back with head to the wall and feet towards the centre of the room (red-ochre burial in E.IV.8 and one burial in VI.B.10). In the shrines and houses of Level VI (A and B) several layers of burials are not uncommon and later burials frequently disturbed the bones of earlier interments. In the later layers less care seems to have been taken not to disturb earlier burials and their bones and skulls are frequently rearranged and funeral gifts scattered. Throughout the Early Neolithic period from Level X to I no change in burial-customs seems to have occurred.

Plate 93

Plate 92

Plate 96

Individual graves are rare. Most houses and shrines served as family burial sites and the longer a building was occupied the greater is the number of bodies found. The maximum number, thirty-two individuals, came from shrine VI.B and A.10, occupied throughout Levels VI B and A, but house VI.B.34 yielded not less than twenty-eight burials. On the other hand shrine VI.61, also occupied in both Levels VI B and VI A, yielded only thirteen and shrine VI.A.25 a single woman and child. It proves impossible to correlate the number of burials, sometimes extending over generations, to the length of occupation of a building and the very small number of

dead found in certain buildings, especially in the lower levels
(IX–VII) or in Level V, makes one wonder where their occupants
were buried. It is for instance inconceivable that only six deaths took
place during the 120 years or so that the great vulture shrine (VII.8)
was used, and this again suggests that shrines were not continually
used as burying places, but may have been reserved for special
individuals only. The same question arises in the case of houses,
where the number of burials seldom suggests that all their occupants
had been buried in the building. Only one house, VI.B.34, with
twenty-eight burials over a period of about a century or four
generations of seven individuals per generation (including small
children) approaches what one would expect, but in all other buildings of Level VI the number is much less (three burials per house for
the entire VI B and A period of about 150 years cannot represent all
the dead). So where are they buried? Only excavation on a much
larger scale might eventually settle this intriguing problem, which at
the moment is insoluble, as a great number of burials in Level VI B
shrines have not yet been excavated. There remains however one
possible solution to account for only 229 skeletons of Level VI (A
and B) in thirteen shrines and eight houses, and that is by assuming
that the dead buried in the shrines are part of the population of the
houses (on the assumption that the shrines were occupied only at
certain times of the year for religious ceremonies). If the 229 burials
are divided over eight houses, the average of 28 dead occurred per
house over six generations (or about 150 years, the estimated length
of Levels VI B and A together). This gives four to five dead per
generation in each house, which agrees with the size of the building,
the sleeping space and hence the average size of a family. This would
mean that more than two-thirds of the population (160 out of 229)
was buried in the shrines, which confirms our opinion that the entire
quarter was inhabited by priests and priestesses, who would naturally
prefer to be buried in hallowed ground. This picture will probably
need modification when excavations are resumed and more burials
are found in shrines and houses of this quarter, so no great reliance
should be placed on the actual numbers of dead here used for calcu-
lation. It would be extremely interesting to compare these results

from the priests quarter with a purely residential area and see if the number of dead buried below the houses is considerably greater. Evidence from the upper levels cannot be used for comparison as there is good reason to show that the area remained a shrine area.

A further point of considerable interest emerges from a study of the skeletons and their burial gifts and that is that those dead buried in shrines or probable shrines are generally better provided for than the dead buried in the houses. This again suggests that the privileged dead buried in the shrines had been people who during life had enjoyed affluence, respect or authority; in fact members of a higher social order or distinction than their relatives buried in the houses. These differences marked as they are, should not be exaggerated; even the burials in a number of shrines were by no means richly equipped, and bordered on poverty (*e.g.* shrines VI.14, 15, 25, 12; VII.1 and 8, etc.). The equipment of the dead was subject to a number of considerations: his status in life, his own wishes, the respect or covetousness of his relatives, possible religious consider-ations, the nature of his death, etc.; in other words factors which no archaeologist can ever hope to distinguish. The greater number of burials in houses and shrines alike were not provided with any gifts.

Out of a total of about 400 skeletons (or parts thereof) only eleven may be singled out as ochre-burials, painted with red ochre or cinnabar (mercury oxide) on the skull or skull and body. Such burials are then far from common, but occur from Levels IX to III almost exclusively in shrines. Moreover, most if not all, appear to have been of the female sex, but, with some exceptions, their funeral gifts, the main item of which was a necklace, are not rich ones by Çatal Hüyük standards. One was a prematurely born infant (VI.A.14), another a mother buried with a child on top of her and accompanied by an adze, a flint dagger with chalk pommel, a spoon and spatula and some fresh water mussels filled with red ochre (VIII.1). A third, a girl of about seventeen who suffered from a broken femur which might have crippled her (IX.1), was treated with red ochre all over the body and had cinnabar applied to the skull as well. With her were several necklaces and some copper and lead beads, the earliest found on the site. Red ochre

Plate 97

also covered the skull and entire upper part of the body of a child (E.IV.8) accompanied by a fine necklace of apatite beads of graded size in the form of highly schematized goddesses, a bone pin and a fine obsidian blade. The skull of a woman with a necklace of sliced dentalium beads (VI.B.20) bore a broad band of brilliant cinnabar paint. Another red ochre burial in shrine E.IV.4 was provided with shells and red painted pebbles.

Green paint was found on three burials in Levels VI and VII; in one case, it covered the bones of a man, in another it had been applied to the eyebrows of a female skull (VI.B.20). More common than green pigment (malachite ?) was a bright blue azurite paint applied to the area around the neck of ten skeletons, male and female in Levels VII and VI. Blue and green apatite beads seem to take the place of these copper carbonate pigments in Levels V and IV. Gifts with the blue- and green-painted burials were rich in comparison to those of the red-ochre ones, but unlike the latter, they were found both in shrines and houses, and were applied to both sexes.

Two groups of objects, never found in houses but confined to burials in shrines, female and male respectively, are mirrors of obsidian (Levels VI B to IV) and bone belt-fasteners, possibly connected with ceremonial leopard-skin dress (Levels VI B, VI A, and III?). Presumably these should be regarded as attributes of certain priestesses and priests, which would explain both their rarity and their discovery in shrines. Fine flint daggers and spouted stone vessels also appear only as gifts in shrines or with male burials beneath shrines.

The variety of funerary gifts gives one a fair picture of the range of objects and materials used in daily life and it may here be noted that no single object seems to have been made exclusively for funerary use. Pottery vessels, figurines of humans, animals or cult-statuettes were never buried with the dead.

All the dead were probably buried in their garments, and wooden bowls, cups and boxes as well as baskets and food, berries, peas, lentils, grain, eggs or a joint of meat are found with the dead irrespective of their sex. Among the other funeral gifts there are marked differences between those that accompany men on the one hand and women and children on the other. Articles of personal ornament are a prerogative of the women. Cosmetic sets containing a small spoon, a fork and a palette; shells filled with red ochre, ointment-sticks of bone, baskets with rouge (red ochre mixed with fat), obsidian mirrors, are exclusively found with women. Jewellery, though not confined to the fair sex, takes the form of necklaces, bracelets, armlets and anklets of beads of a vast variety of stones, shell, clay, bone, animal teeth and, less common, beads of copper and lead. Finger-rings may be made of bone or copper, and wooden pins are sheathed in the same material. Other bracelets are made of marble, alabaster or grey limestone, and there is a collar carved of large boar tusk. Bone pins fastened women's garments near the shoulder. Amulets and pendants are common. Where a woman is buried with a child spoons, spatulae and ladles of bone frequently occur. Tools are less frequent, but include awls for sewing, bodkins for basketry work, knives and hoes. Children have necklaces, pendants, and rings, but otherwise no specific burial gifts.

Male burials show little taste for jewellery. A few beads, pendants, shells or animal teeth may have been worn on a string round the neck, as is also shown in the wall-paintings, but no male was adorned with elaborate necklaces like the women. Instead he was equipped with his weapons; maces with perforated heads of polished stone, daggers, knives and firestones for striking fire of flint (often accompanied by a piece of sulphur). The firestones are frequently found together with a knife and a scraper, all showing a 'pocket sheen', derived from frequent handling with greasy hands, and once carried in a leather bag. On a few occasions a composite tool has been produced that combined all three functions: knife, scraper and fire-stone, the predecessor of our pocket-knife. Groups of arrowheads, single spearheads, a few sickle-blades, knife-blades of obsidian or flint are very often buried with the male dead. Hooks-and-eyes for fastening belts, antler toggles for loin-cloths or cloaks were articles of male dress. Metal, if not altogether absent, with male burials is extremely rare. Baked clay stamp-seals have been found in two graves, but the sex of their owners could not be determined. One male was provided with a ceremonial dagger, a stone bowl, green paint and ointment-sticks and a bone scoop.

Plate XII

Plate 95

Plate 115

X

Crafts and Trade

A GREAT NUMBER of objects used in everyday life have been recovered at Çatal Hüyük, abandoned on the floors of houses as successive settlements burnt, broken or thrown away with the swept-out domestic rubbish, deposited as offerings to the gods in shrines, as funeral-gifts with the dead, or safeguarded in hoards below the floor. Owing to the many fires from which people fled for their lives, the abandoned material is rich and varied, but one specific conflagration, that in which the settlement of Level VI A perished *c.* 5880 BC, fiercer than most, led to the preservation of a quantity of perishable materials, such as cloth, fur, leather, and wood, which are not normally preserved. The terrific heat generated by the burning town, which must have smouldered for a long time, penetrated to a depth of about a metre or more below the level of the floors, carbonising the earth, the bones of the dead and their burial-gifts and arrested all bacterial decay. The scorching heat was enough to destroy most of the cloth in which the dead were wrapped, but it has survived intact below the skeletons.

As a result of this fire much perishable material is available for study and as the fire came at a period in the history of Çatal Hüyük which marked the transition from a society still largely relying on wood and basketry for its vessels instead of pottery (which becomes common only after the fire, in Level V), this unique evidence is extremely valuable. Far too often the archaeologist is forced to evaluate a culture from a few broken pots, and tools and weapons of stone and bone, which may conceivably present a false or incomplete picture. At Çatal Hüyük it is clear that the crafts of the weaver and the woodworker were much more highly esteemed than those of the potter or the bone-carver, and one may well wonder whether these two crafts have not been generally underrated or at least inadequately represented among the achievements of the Neolithic period.

Very few signs of industry have been found in the priestly quarter excavated at Çatal Hüyük, apart from such normal domestic occupations as the preparation of food, the baking of bread and slingstones in ovens, the cutting of wood for fuel, awls for the mending of clothes and bodkins for the repair of mats and basketry; primary occupations which did not need skilled labour.

On the other hand, there is no evidence that any of the more specialized crafts were performed in this quarter—such as the chipping of obsidian tools and weapons, the polishing of stone tools, the drilling and manufacture of beads, the weaving of cloth, etc. The objects found in the houses and shrines of the quarter are all finished products, and the area of the workshops where these items were made, sold or bartered, must lie somewhere else on the mound. The amount of technological specialization at Çatal Hüyük is one of the most striking features of this highly developed society which was obviously in the vanguard of Neolithic progress. The result of this specialization is equally apparent, for the quality and refinement of nearly everything made here is without parallel in the contemporary Near East. The priests and priestesses evidently did not bother to weave their own cloth or chip their own tools, they went to the bazaar and utilized the handiwork of others. Nor did they reap their own grain or spin their wool, and the idea of a home-industry was evidently frowned upon by these elegant sophisticates. Out of over two hundred rooms we have but one sickle and less than a dozen cores of obsidian, a single spindle-whorl and not a single loom-weight. However, there was evidence for fourteen cultivated food-plants, a great deal of cloth and hundreds of finely finished obsidian weapons. Consequently one is better informed about the actual artefacts which these people used than about the technology of their manufacturing processes, many of which remain to be studied. How, for example, did they polish a mirror of obsidian, a hard volcanic glass, without scratching it and how did they drill holes through stone beads (including obsidian), holes so small that no fine modern steel needle can penetrate? When and where did they learn to smelt copper and lead, metals attested at Çatal Hüyük since Level IX, *c* 6400 BC? Did they use coal as fuel as well as for making beads and pendants? These and a host of other questions may only be answered when the workshops are found, and perhaps not even then.

Fig. 1

One of the most fascinating tasks is the location of the sources tapped by Çatal Hüyük for its raw materials, for with the exception of clay, reeds and wood nearly everything used was made from materials not locally available. Even timber for building (oak and juniper) does not grow in the plain, but was brought from the hills and probably floated down the river. Fir, used for carving wooden bowls, was brought from the forests in the Taurus Mountains, so were numbers of foodstuffs. Greenstone and volcanic rocks could be found somewhat nearer, the first on a low ridge between Çumra

Plate II

and Karaman, the latter on the Karadağ, the prominent mountain which dominates the centre of the Konya Plain. In its foothills limestone is also available. Farther east lies a set of volcanoes, still active during the Neolithic period; Mekke Dağ, Karaca Dağ, the twin

Plate I

peaked cone of Hasan Dağ and, farthest away to the north-east, the giant Erciyes Dağ. Obsidian was obtained from some of these volcanoes and it is definitely known to occur on the Karaca and Hasan Dağ, and near the crater lake of Acigöl (Topada). A red obsidian with black streaks occurs in a deposit on the Nevşehir road. Which of these sources provided the obsidian for Çatal Hüyük has not yet been definitely established, but the main source was probably Hasan Dağ. Calcite and alabaster probably came from the Kayseri region, fine white marble from western Anatolia. Stalactites must have been derived from limestone caves known to exist in the Taurus Mountains south and west of the plain. The western hills behind Konya, rich in brightly coloured iron oxides, may have provided a great number of pigments and cinnabar was mined near Sizma, north-west of Konya. The provenances of the copper ores, (cuprite, malachite, azurite), of haematite, limonite, manganese, galena and lignite have not yet been determined, but all these metals are common in the Taurus Mountains. Trade with regions further south is well attested in the form of Mediterranean shells (especially dentalium, but with a sprinkling of cardium, cowrie and whelks), and fine tabular flint, the nearest sources of which lie in the region of Gaziantep, south of the Taurus Mountains. Good flint is unknown on the south Anatolian plateau, but there is some cream, brown, yellow and red chert which was, however, little used at Çatal Hüyük.

The common use of all these rocks and minerals clearly shows that prospecting and trade formed a most important item of the city's economy and undoubtedly contributed appreciably to its wealth and prosperity. The sources of a great number of rocks are still unknown or can only be guessed and in this category fall apatite, rock crystal, carnelian, jasper, chalcedony, and several others.

The stone industries of Çatal Hüyük mark the climax of neolithic chipping and polishing and betray an immensely long ancestry. Certain tools such as the huge scrapers for cleaning hides are ultimately derived from the Middle Palaeolithic flake-industries, whereas the bulk of tools are made in the blade-industry which first appeared in the Upper Palaeolithic at the same time as *Homo Sapiens*. For chipping tools and weapons Neolithic man at Çatal Hüyük made predominant use of black obsidian, derived from the volcanoes whose peaks are visible from the site on a clear day. A certain amount of flint, not locally available, was, however, used and its tougher quality was evidently recognized, for it was employed in the manufacture of daggers with serrated edges, scrapers, firestones (for striking fire) and a small number of knives. The sharper but more brittle obsidian was fashioned into a great number of tools and weapons among which the spearheads, up to 18 cms in length, and two sizes of arrowheads, perhaps suited to a long and short bow, are the finest products. Bifacially pressure-flaked, these weapons rival the finest Solutrean specimens. Unifacial pressure-flaking is found only on the flint daggers which were first ground down to the required thickness and then flaked to produce a serrated cutting edge. These daggers had hilts of wood, sometimes with a pommel of chalk and one particularly fine ceremonial weapon was provided with a hilt of bone carved in the shape of a snake with beady eyes and pointillé incision simulating the reptile's scales. It was fixed to the blade with lime, which may have been mixed with resin, and

54 Ceremonial flint dagger with bone handle. From a male burial in shrine VI.A.29. See Plate XIV

the final fastening was done by means of fine twine wound round the lower part of the hilt. Scrapers of all sizes, knives, sickle-blades, gouges, chisels and a few burins make up the rest of the industry. Picks and hoes are absent, borers or piercers rare in stone, their place being taken by thousands of bone awls. Cores, roughouts and raw material occur in hoards, showing that fabrication was done on the site, though evidently not in the quarter excavated. In the latest levels (III and II) there is a marked decline in the chipped stone industry, which had reached its climax in Levels VII–V, and a few atypical microliths appear. The latter are not only rare, but unusual and without parallel yet their presence does not affect the development of the industry, which is characterized by large tools and is not microlithic. In fact it is already clear that this industry was derived from an earlier one in obsidian, also characterized by large tools as well as by the total absence of microliths.

The polished stone industry is no less developed; obsidian mirrors, carved and polished statuettes, finely ground and perforated mace-heads, fitted with shafts of wood *c.* 63 cms in length, or shorter

Plate 112

shafts of bone; polished stone bowls, cosmetic palettes, and thousands of fine stone beads show a high technological development. Saddle querns, rubbing stones, mortars and pestles, polishing stones, rings of stone, bracelets, grooved stones for polishing bone, greenstone axes, adzes and chisels (and also miniatures of these) for fine woodwork abound. Flint axes and adzes are quite unknown. There appear to have been few stones that the Neolithic people of Çatal Hüyük were not able to work by grinding, polishing and perforating. The notable exceptions are granite, gneiss, basalt, diorite and other hard igneous rocks which were not used.

The same techniques of grinding and polishing were applied to shell and bone, elements of which are frequently combined with

Plates 103, XV

stone beads in necklaces, armlets, bracelets and anklets, where possible in striking and harmoniously blended colour-schemes.

Plate 98

Boar tusk was less commonly used, but when found it is often perforated or ornamented with incised geometric designs.

Bone tools and implements are very common and range from oval cups and scoops to ladles, spatulae, cosmetic tools (spatulae

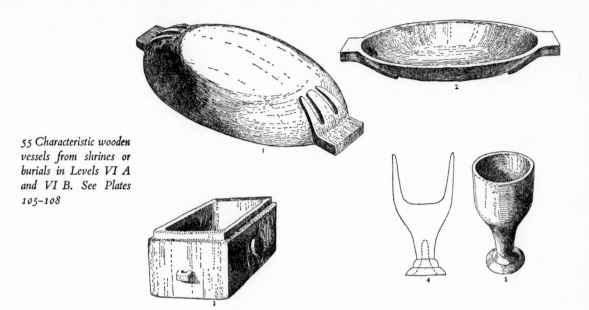

55 Characteristic wooden vessels from shrines or burials in Levels VI A and VI B. See Plates 105–108

ending in little carved hand forks, ointment sticks, etc.), to pins, bodkins, awls, punches and polishers for leather working. Antler toggles and finely polished hooks and eyes for fastening belts have already been mentioned and bone wrist-guards were used by archers. Small bone handles may have held copper awls. Incised decoration is rare on bone tools and ornaments, and in general incision was little practised. Most of the stone tools must have had wooden, rather than bone handles, which explains their rarity. Antler was also fairly rare and was used mainly for toggles and once for making a sickle.

Wood was widely used; trees were cut with polished greenstone axes. Adzes and chisels in the same material, used for carpentry, are abundant and all timber at Çatal Hüyük, oak or juniper, was squared, not only the roof beams and the posts but also the ladders. Wooden vessels were cut with stone tools out of fir and possibly other soft woods. The Neolithic woodworkers created a sophisticated set of wooden vessels: great meat dishes 50 cms in length with carved handles, oval bowls with ledge handles, deep or shallow round bowls and dishes, boat-shaped vessels, sauceboats and an egg-cup. Small boxes occur in many varieties, each with a well-fitting lid. These may be square, oblong or oval and frequently have small lugs, a knob on the lid and sometimes relief decoration. Others again were painted red.

Plates 99, 101, 102

Plate 100

Fig. 55
Plates 106, 108
Plate 107

Plate 105

It is clear from the pottery shapes that throughout the Neolithic period at Çatal Hüyük pottery occupied a secondary position and was unable to free itself completely from hitherto current shapes in wood and basketry. As late as Level II (*c.* 5750–5700 BC) a fair number of pottery shapes are angular and wooden, imitate wooden boxes, or have wooden feet. This shows conclusively that wooden vessels continued to be made side by side with the pottery until the end of the settlement, and there is *à priori* no reason why woodworking should have declined. Generally the importance of ceramic production in the Neolithic has probably been greatly overrated. It was a technological advance like any other and was no doubt useful for cooking, but it was easily breakable, hard to transport, in these early phases not so easy to fire well and aesthetically not very attractive. It is only in the later part of the Neolithic that improved firing conditions led to the production of cream coloured wares, which in the immediately following period, the Early Chalcolithic, were lavishly decorated with painted designs. The few streaks and bands of paint on light coloured pots, that make a sporadic appearance since Çatal Hüyük Level III, showed little promise of the spectacular painted pottery that was to come.

The monochrome Neolithic pottery of Çatal Hüyük is made from a fine grit-tempered clay (usually without any straw). It was built up in coils on a flat base and the walls of the vessel were afterwards thinned out by paddle and anvil method, which involved beating the clay walls with a wooden paddle against a wooden block held inside the pot. When leather hard, the pot was burnished with a piece of bone or a pebble to reduce porosity and produce a fine shine when fired. The firing was apparently done in a bread oven or in a closed kiln with separate firing chamber of which two were found in Level VI. With the exception of a few bowls in Levels IV–II which have simple horizontal incised lines (without white fill) along the rim, the Çatal Hüyük pottery is not decorated. Impressed designs, roulette impressions or combing with the edge of a cardium shell, barbotine pattern, etc., characteristic of a small proportion of the contemporary neolithic pottery of Mersin, Tarsus, Ras Shamra, etc., on the coasts of Cilicia and North Syria, is unknown on the Anatolian

Plateau or on the coast of Pamphylia, where similar Neolithic wares occur in a number of caves and rock-shelters.

The colour of this Çatal Hüyük neolithic pottery varies consider-ably: most of the hole-mouth cooking-pots, exposed to fire, are dark grey or brownish black and a number of bowls show the same colours. Others are red, buff, light grey, beige and orange as early as Levels X and IX, when this pottery is first found. Some of the coarse ware is brick red (Levels X–IX), but it is confined to these early levels. To call this pottery (as has been done) 'Dark burnished ware' or 'Syro-Cicilian' is inaccurate, for much of it is light in colour and its distribution is not confined to the north-eastern corner of the Mediterranean, but includes the entire south Anatolian Plateau.

Plates 109, 110

It is clear that the beginnings of pottery manufacture have not yet been reached at Çatal Hüyük, where it has been found down to Level XIII in 1965. From Level V onwards pottery is regularly found in every house and it gradually increases both in quantity and quality as time goes on. Lighter-coloured wares increase, often with fine mottled surfaces and more elegant shapes and by the end of Level II, *c.* 5700 BC, cream-coloured bowls are com-mon, painting begins and tubular vertically placed lugs make their first appearance. The cooking-pots show little change in shape from Level X to Level I, but their lugs gradually change to crescentic ledge handles. Bases are usually flat, but ring and disc bases occur early and some of the later vessels have four elegant L shaped feet.

Plate 111

Clay balls, baked in ovens, and clay figurines of human beings and animals were common and some of these balls bear incised decoration. Baked clay was also used for the production of beads and pendants, slingstones, stamp-seals and statuettes at least from Level VI B onwards, *i.e.* after 6000 BC.

Particularly interesting is the use of copper and lead, in the form of beads and pendants, tubes and other trinkets, as early as Level IX, *c.* 6400 BC. Finds of copper and lead beads occur in nearly every building-level and it would not be surprising if gold and silver were also known, even though they have not yet been found or recog-nized. A lump of slag from Level VI A has shown upon analysis that copper was being extracted from its ore and the presence of lead,

Plate 104

which occurs in Anatolia as galena, implies smelting as early as Level IX. Other copper beads have been produced from native copper which occurs, for example, in quantity at Ergani Maden, north of Diyarbakir, and probably elsewhere in Anatolia. The presence of a copper awl, 4 cms in length in a stratified position in the lower levels of the village site of Suberde, some fifty miles south-west of Çatal Hüyük at a date roughly comparable to Çatal Hüyük X–VI, throws interesting light on the spread of metal-working even to the villages surrounding the Konya Plain. The beads were made from thin hammered copper sheets rolled up, but it is not yet clear whether heat was applied to facilitate this. Further analyses are in progress.

The evidence for weaving at Çatal Hüyük is manifold; clay or silica imprints of mats and baskets and carbonized remains of the same; wall-paintings showing goddesses in richly coloured and patterned garments, and men in white loin-cloths; statuettes wearing fringed garments and finally numerous fragments of woven cloth, felt, string, thread and rope of plant fibre.

Spirally-worked coiled baskets are common in all levels and in a deposit of grain some actual fragments of thin plant stems, possibly cereal straw, sewn or tied with grass blades, were found in Level IV. The basketry technique used here consisted of taking a continuous strip or bundle of regular thickness of straw or other plant-stems and tying them together in spiral coils by means of bast or other flexible material, so that each turn of the bast around the bundle is connected with the previous ring and finally the straw is completely covered by the bast. In this way it is possible to build up a tight container, just as pottery may be built up from a consecutive series of strips of clay. The two techniques are, in fact, closely related.

Plate 120

Rush carpets covered numerous floors and most are woven in a pattern of quadruple warp and weft of very fine rushes or marsh grass. In the carbonized state the stems are no more than a millimetre thick. Others were coarser. In a number of cases it could be established that the mats were woven with a pattern 'placed diagonally to the outer edge. It is worth noting that the same patterns are woven in mats to this day in the village of the Konya Plain and elsewhere in southern Anatolia.

Baskets were used for a great variety of purposes; for the collection and storage of food, as grain bins, for the safe keeping of mirrors and rouge and as containers for the skeletons of children and even adults. Some were provided with lids.

The fragments of fine woven cloth from the burnt burials of Level VI show great technical skill and have been studied by Mr Harold Burnham of the Department of Textiles in the Royal Ontario Museum. His report is not yet available at the time of writing, so that the notes which follow are of a preliminary nature. Owing to the carbonization of the material we are unfortunately not yet certain whether the fibre used was wool or mohair, perhaps both were used. The possibility that the material was linen, *i.e.* flax fibre, can be discarded as flax was not grown at Çatal Hüyük, nor anywhere else before *c.* 5000 BC, which is far too late for a potential import. The yarn used is two-ply, *i.e.* two spun threads wound around each other. No selvage has been preserved, but there is a fine piece of a twined heading cord on a large fragment of plain tabby weave, found inside a human skull. Whereas most of the pieces show a fine plain weave, there are others with a widely spaced weft, producing a shawl-like textile. Still others show knotting resembling a fish-net pattern. Cloth tapes are also found and a young woman buried in shrine VI.A.25 wore a string skirt, the ends of which were encased in small copper tubes for weighting it. Fringes are also commonly found and a small statuette from Level II shows a short skirt with a fringe above and below. One piece of cloth was mended and the sewn edge was clearly visible; the stitch was rather coarse.

Plate 118
Plate 116
Plate 117
Plate 87

All the cloth being carbonized, no traces of colour have survived, but as several of the goddess reliefs show brightly coloured and patterned garments, such must have existed. Evidence for red thread has survived in a number of broken beads, the perforations of which are still stained red. As there was no red ochre present in the grave, this colour must have come from the thread. The abundance of kilim patterns painted on the walls of shrines likewise suggests that gaudily coloured woven rugs were as common a feature of the Neolithic period in Anatolia as they are now. All this evidence suggests that dyeing was well known and some of the commonest weeds in the neighbourhood of Çatal Hüyük are madder (*Rubia tinctorum*), woad (*Isatis tinctoria*) and weld (*Reseda luteola*), which yield a deep red, a blue and a strong yellow respectively. Bedstraw, dock and others, also found in the plain, are well known dye-producing plants. The numerous stamp-seals of baked clay bearing intricate designs of spirals and meanders on shapes which include quatrefoils or flowers and human hands, may have been used to stamp patterns on cloth and need not have been used solely to paint the human skin. None retain any traces of colour, which is not surprising, for a vegetable dye is more subject to decay than the mineral pigments of the wall-paintings. That cloth was indeed stamped with coloured patterns is suggested by some wall-paintings in shrine III.8 which includes numerous quatrefoils, or those of Early Chalcolithic Can Hasan decorated with pseudo-meanders like many of our seals. Already appearing in Level VI, the most elaborately decorated ones derive from Levels IV, III and II.

Plate 121; Fig. 56

Apart from garments of woven cloth, animal-skins and fur were certainly worn as is indicated by numerous wall-paintings, statuettes and fragments in the graves. Leopard-skins were particularly in favour, a fashion that has lasted to the present day. Bonnets were worn, but we have no evidence for footwear, which was probably made of leather and much needed on the snow-covered wintry plateau. Belts were probably made of the same material, but no fragments have survived; however, one dagger was still found in its leather sheath. Tanning may have been known for acorns, brought from the hills, are numerous. Slings were probably of leather and bowstrings were probably made from animal gut.

The excellent preservation of perishable materials at this site offers great hopes for further interesting finds when the excavations can be continued.

56 Stamp seals of baked clay with decorative patterns from Levels VI–II. See Plate 121

The People and their Economy

THE BASIS FOR the spectacular development of the Neolithic at Çatal Hüyük was evidently laid by efficiently organized food production and conservation. That the Neolithic people of this site had successfully established their 'Neolithic Revolution' which meant freedom from hunger, is proved by abundant evidence. In fact, few other sites have preserved such an abundance and variety of foodstuffs and from the sheer size of the as yet uninvestigated aceramic Neolithic mound it is reasonable to conjecture that the same sort of conditions which we find from *c.* 6500 BC (Level X) onwards had prevailed for at least a millennium before, if not considerably earlier. We are still ignorant of the ecological factors involved in the establishment of the first settlement in the plain, in an area which, as Dr Hans Helbaek has shown, cannot have provided by any stretch of imagination the wild progenitor of all forms of barley, the two-row *Hordeum spontaneum* or the progenitor of emmer, *Triticum dicoccoides*. Everything indicates that the plant husbandry of Çatal Hüyük must have a long prehistory somewhere else, in a region where the wild ancestors of these plants were at home, presumably in hilly country, well away from the man-made environment of the Konya Plain. If we may theorize for a little, this statement of the eminent palaeobotanist implies that agriculture was introduced into the plain, not just before Level X, about the middle of the seventh millennium, but much earlier at the time when Çatal Hüyük was founded. Such agricultural beginnings must have started long before the moment at which the first carbonized remains of grains and small legumes make their appearance in the settlements of the Near East, around 7000 BC at aceramic Hacılar 5 in Anatolia, at Beidha VI near Petra and in the Bus Mordeh period of the settlement of Alikosh on the edge of the lowlands of Khuzistan. Even those simple patterns of agriculture show a consistent specialization with hulled two-row barley as the main crop, emmer (*Triticum dicoccum*) cultivated or wild, coming second, some wild einkorn, lentils, pea or vetch as legumes and pistachio and acorns. The beginnings must be sought in the Natufian of Palestine, the still unknown earlier aceramic of the Anatolian Plateau, and in Khuzistan. This will take one into a 'Protoneolithic' period which began at the end of the Pleistocene, archaeologically speaking just after the end of the Upper Palaeolithic.

No study has been made of the ecological and climatic conditions prevailing at the end of the Upper Palaeolithic on the Anatolian Plateau, but J. Birman informed the author in 1963 that he had found definite evidence on the Anatolian Plateau, including the mountain ranges of the Taurus which surround the Konya Plain, for a Last Glacial relapse and a minor readvance of ice during the Younger Dryas of Western Europe (*c.* 8850–8300 BC). K. W. Butzer in his *Environment and archaeology* (Chicago, 1964, pp. 425–6), argues that this final cold period probably did not pass unnoticed in the Near East, producing for example, evidence for moister climate in Palestine and Egypt during part or all of the Natufian period. The rather modest temperature changes (1–3° C) would not have been significant for human habitation, but the depression of the snow line may have had its effect on the distribution of wild cereals which may have been excluded from certain regions. Modern conditions would not have prevailed until *c.* 8000 BC, which is very much the same time-range that may be indicated for the beginnings of agriculture in Anatolia at the end of the Palaeolithic. This period saw not only the first establishment of the 'Protoneolithic' village of Jericho, dated by C-14 before 8000 BC but also of contact with Anatolia, from which the first obsidian was exported to Jericho, a contact that was maintained throughout the eighth millennium (Jericho Pre-pottery Neolithic A). Perhaps the first agricultural settlements started to appear in Anatolia as in Palestine after *c.* 8300 BC, perhaps in the eastern hill-zone beyond the Konya Plain where lie the sources of obsidian. This is, of course, pure speculation, not as yet based on any firmly established facts, but the practices of early agriculture, the traditional wooden-house architecture of Çatal Hüyük, and likewise the commercial and perhaps ritual importance of obsidian may point to this hilly region.

The conquest of the plain must, as Helbaek has pointed out, come later. Its exact date is unknown, but man by then was able to introduce agriculture into a new environment, where seeds were sown in the flood pools of the Çarşamba river which drains from the great mountain lakes of Beyşehir and Suğla into the fertile alluvial plain around Çumra. As late as 6000 BC the Konya Plain teemed with wild life and both the zoologists who have studied our material, Dexter Perkins Jr and Pierre Ducos regard the plain as a favourable ecological niche which produced maximum size in such species as aurochs (*Bos primigenius*), a pig (*Sus scrofa*) and Red Deer (*Cervus elaphus*). Perhaps it was the presence of great herds of these desirable animals that attracted man to the grasslands of the plain. However that may be, considerable ecological differences are marked in the seventh millennium BC between the animals of the plain and those living round the intramontane lake of Suğla near Seydişehir, as revealed by the recent excavations of J. Bordaz at the village site of Suberde. Here 90 per cent of the animal-bones belonged to wild sheep, pig and Red Deer, the remaining 10 per cent being aurochs, goat, wolf, fox and tortoise. A small race of pigs, different from the gigantic species of the Konya Plain, is perhaps the only animal that may have been domesticated. At Çatal Hüyük on the other hand domestic sheep and goat occur even in the lowest layers, but pigs are not domesticated and the possibility of domestication of the aurochs cannot yet be proved statistically. In the microlithic obsidian and flint industry of Suberde the great hunting weapons of Çatal Hüyük are conspicuous by their absence and even the arrowheads are different. Evidently the hunting of large game was less a feature of Neolithic life in this village than it was at Çatal Hüyük where the main quarry was formed by the herds of aurochs, wild pig, and Red Deer. Two species of wild ass, wild sheep, Roe Deer, Fallow Deer, an occasional gazelle, fox, wolf, and leopards were also hunted. No bones of lion have yet been found, but there may be some bear. A wall-painting is not the only evidence for domestic dog. Birds and fish were also caught but they were obviously less prized; of snails there is no trace. The people of Çatal Hüyük then made good use of the hunter's paradise of the Konya Plain and it is of interest to note that, as time went on, it became more and more difficult to find large horn-cores for ritual purposes. The horns used after Level V are very small compared to the enormous ones so common in Levels VII and VI. The same rarity of large specimens may have led to a reduction in the size of spearheads and arrowheads which is notable after Level V and finally to the decline of the stone industry in Levels III and II after which incidentally, the wall-paintings disappear.

Compared to the simple agricultural products of aceramic Hacılar 5, enormous progress was made at Çatal Hüyük during the seventh millennium. By Level VI, *c.* 6000 BC, not less than fourteen food-plants were cultivated. Many more species have been identified, but those mentioned here are the economically important ones. The principal crops were emmer, einkorn, naked six-row barley and pea, all occurring in great quantities from Levels VI–II. Bread-wheat (*Triticum aestivum*) also makes its first appearance in Çatal Hüyük VI. The field pea was more common than the purple pea (*Pisum elatius*) and lentil. A species of vetch (*Vicia noena*) and cultivated bitter vetch (*Ervum ervilia*) also appear in Level VI. Two cruciferous plants, Shepherd's Purse (*Capsella bursapastoris*) and the salt-loving *Erysimum sisymbrioides* were grown as sources of plant fat equivalent to the gathering and cultivation of linseed in more easterly areas at a later date. Among fruit seeds brought from the hills, presumably the Taurus Mountains in the south, were almonds, acorns, pistachio (*Pistacia atlantica*), apple, juniper and hackberry (*Celtis australis*). The latter occurring even in the deepest levels of Çatal Hüyük, was apparently used for making wine. Many weeds provide indications of the conditions prevailing in the Konya Plain some eight thousand years ago and salt-loving species already show that salinity was a feature of the Çumra area as it is now.

It may be of interest to speculate about other kinds of food. Beverages such as beer and wine were evidently known, but grapes and olives do not appear to have been domesticated till the fourth or even third millennium. The acid in the caps of acorns is used today to start the process of making yoghurt, and domestic sheep and goats were evidently kept for their milk and fleece as much as for their meat. When butter and cheese, sour buttermilk or *ayran* were invented we shall probably never know, but they may well be Neolithic. Salt, a necessity in the preparation of vegetable foods, was easy enough to find in the Konya Plain and the Neolithic station of Ilıcapınar on a small salt-lake to the south-west of the Tuz Gölü may have been a trading post specializing in salt export. The paintings of insects hovering over fields of flowers conceivably suggests that honey was known. Other sweetening agents are to this day extracted from the bark of trees by nomads in southern Anatolia. Resins and birch bark may have been used for fastening tools and weapons on to shafts and into handles; bitumen is unknown on the Anatolian plateau.

Of the Neolithic population of Çatal Hüyük nothing definite can be said until the skeletons have been studied by Mlle Denise Ferembach and Professor Lawrence Angel. The following preliminary notes are derived from the observations of Mr D. Biernoff. The population of Çatal Hüyük appears to have been of two different races (recognized by Mlle Ferembach), dolichocephalic Proto-Mediterranean and another brachycephalic element, and of fairly tall stature. The average for women being between 5ft and 5ft 4ins, that for men between 5ft 4ins and 5ft 10ins with few individuals in the extreme brackets. Few people seem to have been more than forty years old. There are no individuals among the burials that showed signs of violent death, nor is any skull trephined. A few individuals show broken limbs, signs of arthritis and caries of the teeth. On the whole, however, dentition is excellent. Childbirth, fevers, and pneumonia are suggested as the main causes of death, not degenerative diseases. Among the skeletons women and children far outnumber men. These observations are subject to confirmation.

Not much can be said about the Neolithic social structure as the excavations have revealed only the religious quarter. The position of women was obviously an important one in an agricultural society with a fertility cult in which a goddess was the principal deity. Social inequality is suggested by sizes of buildings, equipment and burial gifts, but this is never a glaring one. Full-time specialization is fairly obvious and the workshops lay elsewhere on the mound. The variety of arts and crafts practised at Çatal Hüyük is nearly as great as that of the developed civilizations of the Early Bronze Age. Only the arts of book-keeping or writing and music are not represented among the finds. The existence of an ordered pattern of society is evident from the stereotyped house plans, from the standard features and equipment and a strong conservatism is shown by the frequent rebuildings on the same plan, the strict architectural layout and the very few changes that can be observed in the culture over a period of some eight hundred years.

In contrast to other contemporary Neolithic cultures, Çatal Hüyük preserved a number of traditions that seem archaic in a fully developed Neolithic society. The art of wall-painting, the reliefs modelled in clay or cut out of the wall-plaster, the naturalistic representations of animals, human figures and deities, the occasional use of finger-impressed clay designs like 'macaroni,' the developed use of geometric ornament including spirals and meanders, incised on seals or transferred to a new medium of weaving; the modelling of animals wounded in hunting-rites, the practice of red-ochre burials, the archaic amulets in the form of a bird-like steatopygous goddess, and finally certain types of stone tools and the preference for dentalium shells in jewellery, all preserve remains of an Upper Palaeolithic heritage. To a greater or lesser extent, such archaic elements are also traceable in a number of other post-Palaeolithic cultures, such as the Natufian of Palestine, but nowhere are they so pronounced as in the Neolithic of Çatal Hüyük. The reason for the continuance of such Upper Palaeolithic practices there may be due to a strong conservatism but one suspects that it had its origin in the very important part that hunting continued to play in the economy of the Konya Plain. In view of all these survivals one is inclined to believe that this civilization is descended from an Upper Palaeolithic, probably Anatolian, of which hardly anything is known. It would be premature to speculate further about the ancestry of Çatal Hüyük until excavation has been carried further, nor would a comparison with contemporary cultures in the Near East be of any profit as long as so much intervening territory remains to be explored, and other key-sites remain unpublished. To describe the impact of this Neolithic civilization on its neighbours and successors, both in Anatolia and the adjacent countries of south-eastern Europe would demand another volume. Dr Hans Helbaek is now in a position to show that it was the agricultural development of Neolithic Anatolia that was responsible for the spread of agriculture into Europe, preparing the way for the beginning of European civilization which is our common heritage.

Seen in this light, the Neolithic civilization of Çatal Hüyük represents something unique in the long history of human endeavours: a link between the remote hunters of the Upper Palaeolithic and the new order of food-production that was the basis of all our civilization.

Our task is not yet done; at least a decade of continuing work lies ahead. It is to be hoped that, with the co-operation of the Turkish authorities, the excavation of the earliest town of Anatolia and one of the earliest in the world, may shortly be resumed. Meanwhile, something of that town's remarkable quality is here presented as a foretaste of further discovery.

Bibliography

James Mellaart. Excavations at Çatal Hüyük, 1961. First preliminary report. In *Anatolian Studies*, XII, 1962, pp. 41–65; pls III–XVIII.

— Excavations at Çatal Hüyük, 1962. Second preliminary report. In *Anatolian Studies*, XIII, 1963, pp. 43–103; pls III–XXIX.

— Excavations at Çatal Hüyük, 1963. Third preliminary report. In *Anatolian Studies*, XIV, 1964, pp. 39–119; pls I–XXVI.

— Excavations at Çatal Hüyük. 1965. Fourth preliminary report. In *Anatolian Studies*, XVI, 1966, pp. 165–191; pls XXIX–LXIII.

Perry A. Bialor. The chipped stone industry of Çatal Hüyük. In *Anatolian Studies*, XII, 1962, pp. 67–110.

Hans Helbaek. Textiles from Çatal Hüyük. In *Archaeology*, Spring 1963, pp. 39–46.

— First impressions of the Çatal Hüyük plant husbandry. In *Anatolian Studies*, XIV, 1964, pp. 121–3.

H. Neuninger, R. Pittioni and W. Siegl. Frühkeramikzeitliche Kupfergewinnung in Anatolien. In *Archaeologia Austriaca*, 35, 1964, pp. 98–110.

Theodore A. Wertime. Man's first encounters with metallurgy. In *Science*, Dec. 4, 1964, vol. 146. no. 3649, pp. 1257–67.

K. W. Butzer. *Environment and archaeology*. Aldine Co. Chicago, 1964.

Jacques Bordaz. Anatolian Research project. Suberde Excavations, First campaign, Summer 1964. In *New York University, Department of Classics Bulletin* 1964–2 (Nov. 12, 1964).

J. R. Cann and Colin Renfrew. The characterisation of obsidian and its application to the Mediterranean region. In *Proceedings of the Prehistoric Society*, new series XXX, 1964, pp. 111–33; especially pp. 122–3.

H. Burnham. Çatal Hüyük–the textiles and twine fabrics. In *Anatolian Studies*, XV, 1965, pp. 169–74.

List of Illustrations

All photographs, unless otherwise acknowledged, are by Mrs M. A. Mellaart. Reconstructions and line drawings are by Grace Huxtable (G.H.) and Anne-Louise Stockdale (A.-L.S.).

Index